Greenhill Books

THE MAKING OF THE
SAS
AND THE WORLD'S ELITE FORCES

THE MAKING OF THE SAS AND THE WORLD'S ELITE FORCES

DR TERRY WHITE

First published in the US in 1994 by
Greenhill Books, Lionel Leventhal Limited
Park House, 1 Russell Gardens,
London NW11 9NN
and
Stackpole Books
5067 Ritter Road
Mechanicsburg, PA 17055, USA

Library of Congress Cataloging-in-Publication
Data available

ISBN 1-85367-184-3

Editorial and design: Brown Packaging Limited,
255-257 Liverpool Road, London N1 1LX

First published in Great Britain in 1992 as
The Making of the World's Elite Forces
by Sidgwick & Jackson Limited

Printed by Vincenzo Bona, Torino, Italy

CONTENTS

ELITES IN HISTORY

Commanders throughout history have sought to establish special units within their armies which could shatter an opponent's troops in battle. However, as the nature of warfare has changed, so has the role of elite forces.

THE concept of elite fighting units is by no means a modern idea. Throughout history armies have contained units that by reason of superior training and equipment, or perhaps for no better reason than extensive combat experience, are considered outstanding. Persia's Immortals, Alexander the Great's Companion Cavalry, Renaissance Switzerland's pikemen, Napoleon's Imperial Guard and Britain's Guards Regiments are clearly entitled to their elite status. Although separated by thousands of years, they have something in common: they each formed the dependable, potentially battle-winning corps of their respective armies. Their very dependability, their willingness to remain steadfast under heavy fire and then launch attacks to punch their way through an enemy's lines, made them an invaluable asset to any commander. Napoleon fully appreciated the potential of his Guard units, often husbanding them in reserve until the enemy had been fixed in position and battered by his more 'expendable' line units.

The nineteenth century, however, saw a re-evaluation of the role of elite forces, often in the face of some very painful experiences that overturned many long-standing conventional military wisdoms. Previously elites had fought as an integral part of an army on the battlefield and, equally importantly, in a conventional manner. Napoleon's Imperial Guard attempted a standard column attack against the

A regiment of Napoleon's Old Guard, surrounded by British artillery and infantry, is called upon to surrender by General Hill at Waterloo. Refusing, they were decimated by grapeshot.

British Guards at Waterloo (18 June 1815) who, in their turn, defeated the attack with conventional volley fire and bayonet charge. Even at this stage, however, the nature of elite units and their roles were evolving. The British had used locally-raised bands of skilled woodsmen, such as Rogers' Rangers, to take on the French and Indians in north America in the mid-eighteenth century, and were later forced to create permanent units of light infantry from the flank companies of regular regiments to deal with enemy sharpshooters in the American War of Independence (1775-83). Although the structure, tactics and deployment of such units were in part determined by local geography (dense forest bisected by deep gullies that precluded the European-style linear battlefield deployments), they also amounted to tacit recognition that conventional wars can be won, or at least significantly affected by, unconventional means. In contrast to previous elites, these forces, like the rifle-equipped regiments that accompanied the Duke of Wellington's polyglot army in the Peninsular Campaign in Spain (1808-14), consisted of highly skilled individuals who, unlike

Above: Berdan's Sharpshooters in action against Confederate infantry during the Union Army's advance on Vicksburg, May 1863.

their predecessors and most of their contemporaries, were allowed to fight independently and to display individual initiative in combat.

To many less imaginative members of the military's upper echelons, these 'freelance' units were aberrations, to be disbanded or brought to heel after the wars were over. Most European armies of the nineteenth century continued to have elite units, but only in the traditional sense of the idea. Impetus for the development of new types of elite units would come from the 'New' rather than the 'Old' World. The American Civil War (1861-65), a conflict rather looked down upon by Europeans for the use of largely 'undisciplined' conscript armies, saw the emergence of elites which had more in common with Rogers' Rangers than Napoleon's Imperial Guard. The US 1st Infantry Regiment, better known as Berdan's Sharpshooters, did not fight as regulars who deployed in line to exchange volleys with similarly-deployed Confederate units. Rather, they fought as individuals or in small groups, their role to snipe at enemy officers or other high-value targets. Marksmanship, together with accurate long-range rifled muskets, certainly marked them as an elite.

The Confederacy raised a number of 'raiding' forces under men such as John Mosby and Nathan Bedford Forrest. These mounted units were lightly equipped and operated away from the main Southern armies, striking at will against vulnerable points along the North's extensive supply and communications network.

The lessons of the American Civil War were not readily taken to heart by the various European chiefs of staff, who at the end of the nineteenth century were, to all intents and purposes, still deploying their armies according to Napoleonic tactics. However, wartime experience, particularly for the British, was to prompt radical reappraisals of established doctrine. The Second Boer War (1899-1902), much as the First (1880-81), saw the British outmanoeuvred and outshot by Afrikaans-speaking farmers. Columns of British and Commonwealth in-

fantry and cavalry slogged across the *veldt* after an elusive enemy that, in action, fought from trenches and used accurate, aimed shots to cut down rank after rank of slow-moving British units as they marched across the often featureless terrain. Losses, particularly in Black Week (when the British lost three battles in succession), caused a national outcry and forced a rethink of British tactics.

Troopers went into battle in small, tight-knit units

In response, the British deployed Imperial Yeomanry units, predominantly from Australia, New Zealand and Canada. Mounted, lightly equipped, their ranks filled with hardy and skilled frontiersmen who were often the equal of the Boers in marksmanship, the yeomanry chased and harried the Boers as never before and undoubtedly helped in their defeat.

This experience in the Boer War was of great importance to the British Army, and the idea of rapid but aimed rifle fire stood the British Expeditionary Force (BEF) in good stead during the opening months of World War I, though the idea of individual initiative was still very much frowned upon. It was the Imperial German Army in the latter stages of the war, however, that created the first truly elite units (at least in the modern sense). Operation 'Michael', the last-ditch attempt to cut through the Allied lines around Amiens in the spring of 1918, saw the large-scale use of stormtroopers for the first time. These units, filled with veterans, enjoyed the luxuries of better food, pay, training and equipment. Troopers went into battle in small, tight-knit units, carrying plentiful supplies of grenades and, in some cases, the first truly effective submachine gun, the MP18. Unlike regular units, which were supposed to capture whole trench sectors in succession, their role was to probe for points of weakness in the enemy line following a short but devastating bombardment, break through the enemy line and by-pass points of resistance. Follow-on units dealt with strongly defended positions

Left: A Boer War Imperial Yeomanry trooper. These soldiers were highly skilled in raiding techniques.

while the stormtroopers pushed ever deeper into the rear areas to spread confusion and dislocate any attempts at a coordinated response. In essence, this was what later, in World War II, became known as *blitzkrieg* (lightning war).

Initiative was clearly a key component in the practice of *blitzkrieg*

Blitzkrieg, a strategy based on the ideas of Broad, Fuller and Liddell Hart and refined by Heinz Guderian, demanded a great deal of often quite junior officers at the end of a long chain of command, who would have to execute orders in a rapidly changing and highly volatile battlefield situation. Initiative was clearly a key component in the practice of *blitzkrieg* at all levels. Other units, notably airborne forces and special forces, operating in a vital 'spearheading' role, paved the way for the main assault. The defeat of France and her allies in the summer of 1940 was significantly contributed to by the swift successes of a handful of special forces. The airborne landing on the Belgian fortress of Eben Emael by a highly trained band of paratroopers was a textbook operation by an elite force, as was the seizure of a railway bridge over the River Gennep in Holland by Brandenburger troops disguised as Dutch military police. Later in the war, German units would

be involved in a variety of what are now seen as classic examples of elite force exploits: the rescue of Mussolini from his mountain-top prison at Gran Sasso in Italy (September 1943); and the use of American-speaking Brandenburger units to sabotage bridges and communications lines in advance of the German forces during the Ardennes offensive of late 1944.

If Germany led the way in the field of elite forces, Britain and the United States were not far behind. In Britain, in part thanks to the enthusiasm of Winston Churchill, a plethora of both large and small units were raised to strike back at occupied Europe. Army and Royal Marine Commandos, paratroopers and a variety of specialised naval units, all fighting under the umbrella of Combined Operations, launched scores of raids, notable among them being Bruneval (February 1942), St Nazaire (March 1942), Dieppe (August 1942) and the pre-invasion operations on the Normandy coastline. In north Africa, the Special Air Service Regiment under David Stirling and the Long Range Desert Group (LRDG) under David Lloyd-Owen helped to undermine the Axis powers' ability to fight by hitting targets behind the front line. Units raised in the United States, such as the

Below: German stormtroopers attacking British trenches during Ludendorff's July 1918 offensive.

Above: German glider-borne forces after their capture of Eben Emael, May 1940. The man in the hat is a disguised Brandenburger soldier.

Rangers and paratroopers, went on to play vital spearheading roles in the invasions of north Africa, Italy, France and Germany, as well as contributing to victory in the Pacific.

The end of World War II saw the run down of many of these elite forces. However, in Africa and Asia the process of de-colonisation resulted in a number of small-scale wars against nationalist/communist guerrilla groups seeking independence from their former colonial rulers. Conventional forces took part in these 'brush-fire' wars, often with considerable success, but it was recognised that their training and techniques were not ideal in the circumstances. What were required were units schooled in the arts of guerrilla warfare, units capable of meeting the enemy on their own terms.

Specialist training was developed in the areas of weapons skills, survival, communications, medicine and general 'hearts and minds' techniques. Britain's SAS showed the value of extensive training in unconventional warfare skills during their campaigns in Malaya, Borneo, Aden and Oman. The US Green Berets were specifically raised to cope with Viet Cong guerrillas in Vietnam by winning the confidence of local tribesmen.

More recently, special forces have had to prepare to meet a new type of war: terrorism. Consequently, elite units such as the SAS,

Delta Force, Germany's GSG 9 and France's GIGN have been specifically created to counter the threat, or have taken on the responsibility. The overt operations of World War II and before have now given way, at least in part, to the shadowy world of covert operations in which the violence of events, such as the storming of the Iranian Embassy in London in May 1980, are only a small part of the whole story. Intelligence gathering, rigorous training and selection, and international cooperation count for much in the war against terrorism.

Today's elite forces are not the professional heart and backbone of armies. Although they do operate with highly trained conventional forces, their role is much more varied than solely fighting on a battlefield. They are taught to carry out raids, to conduct hostage-rescue missions and, above all, to operate in small, self-contained groups. As the 1991 Gulf War demonstrated, these units are very capable in this role. But, as the continuing operations in Northern Ireland and Central America also show, they are flexible enough to fight in the twilight world of low-intensity campaigns that is neither outright peace nor outright war.

SELECTION AND TRAINING

Selection procedures for elite units are tough to ensure that only those recruits with great mental and physical stamina get through. They are men who will keep on going when others want to give up, and who have the aptitude to operate sophisticated hardware.

UNITS such as the British SAS, US 'Green Berets' and SEALs and Soviet *spetsnaz* forces have set standards of excellence for special forces. As a result, selection and training methods, though having unique aspects due to unit roles, have many similarities the world over. These processes are also tightly controlled. It was not always so. In World War II, for example, the men of the Long Range Desert Group were selected by interview and then underwent a short period of training during subsequent operations; and recruits to David Stirling's SAS faced a tiring 48km night march across the desert or a timed run over a nearby hill before acceptance.

Back in Britain, however, the newly raised commandos and paratroops had the time and facilities to take the business of selection and training very seriously. The Royal Marine Commandos set up a permanent training establishment at Achnacarry in Scotland, where aerial assault courses were made all the more difficult by live machine-gun fire and explosive charges detonated close to various obstacles.

Prospective recruits to Britain's 5 Airborne Brigade's Pathfinder Platoon undergoing selection at Okehampton in Devon. Only the best are accepted for Britain's spearhead unit.

Similar realism was used for the small-boat landings in a nearby loch, but the risk of injury, or even death, in training was no more than the men could expect on their first raid.

Realism was also the hallmark of the training of units such as the British and American airborne forces. The nucleus of the British Parachute Regiment was drawn initially from the experienced and courageous men of No 2 Commando, deceptively titled No 11 Special Air Service Battalion to confuse the enemy. Lieutenant-Colonel Otway's official history of the airborne forces records their selection and training: 'These men were tough, but even so all of them could not manage parachuting. Of the total number who were accepted from the original No 2 Commando, 30 refused to jump, two were killed through parachute failures and 20 others were found unsuitable or sustained medical injuries.' In his book *Prelude to Glory*, Group Captain Newnham was more explicit: 'Most of the men were of a good type and were a loss to the Commando. The majority got to the edge of the hole in the aircraft before refusing. Four men fainted in the aircraft, while a number jumped in a state of collapse having forced themselves to do so by sheer willpower.' This rather harsh form of selection was necessary. Both the commandos and paratroops faced the enemy in small, lightly armed groups. If a man froze at the moment of leaving an aircraft or boat, it could endanger the entire operation.

Above: A British para recruit on the Trainasium, an obstacle course designed to see whether a man has 'what it takes' to jump out of an aircraft.

Today's elite units attempt to select their men without losing any of them in the process. Fatalities have, however, occurred on some selection and training courses, notably during SAS winter selection and various resistance to interrogation exercises, but these incidents have been held up to both internal and public scrutiny, and training methods changed if required. In the current economic climate, selection and training must be cost-effective and all candidates must be given the necessary opportunity to show the selectors that they have what it takes to be a para, Green Beret or SAS trooper.

Most modern elite units fight in small, independent groups

For their part, the selectors are looking for two main sets of qualities. The first is required of all battlefield elites: aggression, physical fitness and *esprit de corps*. The second set of qualities is role orientated. Most modern elite units fight in small, independent groups either at the forefront of the battle or behind enemy lines. Such men must have a high degree of self-discipline, motivation, native intelligence and initiative. In combat they must be dependable, self-reliant and masters of an array of modern equipment, weapons, field tactics and many other specialised skills needed for their work.

The two biggest hurdles facing an applicant for an elite unit are, first, plucking up the courage to 'have a go' and, second, remaining on selection when the going starts to get tough. The going gets tough quickly for new arrivals at the Parachute Regiment's Depot in Aldershot. They leave the comforts of 'civvie street', the right to do what they want when they want, and a familiar pattern of life. In return, recruit training offers an iron regime that starts at 0700 hours and ends at 2000 hours, when the course is finally stood down — 13 hours of basic soldiering and fitness training designed to bring the recruits close to the minimum personal standard required to pass selection.

In reality, the day does not finish when the course is stood down. The recruits' notebooks

Below: A para Stretcher Race, only this stretcher is made of steel and feels like it weighs a tonne. What's worse, the recruits have to run with it.

are full of memos taken during the welcome breaks for lessons on unfamiliar details about infantry weapons and kit that needs to be memorised. There are lockers to be tidied, boots to be highly polished and uniforms to be washed and pressed. Finally, they prepare their kit for the next morning. For the first time in their lives they are faced with paying for what they lose. Much worse is the threat of having to explain the loss at the next kit inspection, or going on a field exercise without an essential item of kit such as a piece of webbing or water bottle. All transgressions invite the unwelcome attentions of the instructors. At best, they can expect public ridicule together with an impossible number of press-ups. At worst, their 'card is marked' by the selectors — their status becomes 'doubtful'. Sunday becomes more than a rest day, it marks the end of yet another week completed.

The recruits' worst enemy at this stage of their training is the knowledge that they can leave at any time. Up until Week Eight all recruits have the right to be discharged for the nominal fee of £100. Many take up that right. The final straw might come on a wet night in the field when, already exhausted, they are woken up at 0200 hours to take their turn on 'stag' (guard duty), or when a 16km speed march continues past the usual finishing point and onto the assault course.

The recruits are immediately marched onto the course 'black-spot'

At the end of Week Four, the survivors 'pass off the square' and on to the endurance phase of P-Company. Now only the motivated remain, thoughts of leaving are gone — ahead lies the famous Red Beret. 'Basic Wales' not only continues to develop the recruits' infantry skills but also concentrates on the men's character and motivation, with speed marches across the Welsh hills interspersed with adventure training. After a brief interlude on the ranges to test the recruits' marksmanship and weapons handling, Week 12 or 'Test Week' arrives all too quickly.

On the Friday morning the recruits face the 'Steeplechase' — a test of individual effort and

most of the way to complete this test in the satisfactory time of 105 minutes. Already exhausted, the recruits are immediately marched onto the course 'black-spot'. The Trainasium is a structure of scaffolding poles and narrow catwalks, 7-15m high and cunningly constructed to test the recruit's nerve and reaction to orders. After leaping gaps, crawling across wires and standing unaided on the 15m 'shuffle-bars', the recruits face a standing jump across a 2.5m gap. On each obstacle the recruit is given just three opportunities to overcome his fear and natural inclinations, a mental process that he will need to repeat every time he arrives at the open door of an aircraft.

The students make practice jumps from the indoor descent trainer

This phase of P-Company ends with the assault course, after which the recruits are treated to further endurance marches and a stretcher race across the forbidding hills of the Brecon Beacons. Now the recruit has his 'Red Beret' and is despatched to the Royal Air Force's No 1 Parachute School to earn his wings. In the almost relaxed atmosphere of RAF Brize Norton, the novice paratroopers learn to land correctly and cope with several types of potentially fatal mid-air emergencies. After becoming acquainted with the PX1 Mks IV and V main parachutes and the PR7 reserve, the students make practice jumps from the indoor descent trainer and the 22m tower, before steeling themselves for the hated balloon jump. Aircraft drills, mock exits and the outdoor exit-trainer — designed to simulate an aircraft's 160km/hr slipstream — prepare the course for the main event. Weather permitting, at the end of 20 days of training the men have completed eight aircraft descents, including jumps at night and under operational conditions. Ahead lies more advanced infantry training with their battalions. After 2-3 years experience in a rifle company, there is the possibility of further specialised training with the numerous support platoons and sections, or

physical fitness. To pass, a recruit must twice negotiate a 1.3km obstacle circuit in an average time of 17.5 minutes. The next event is a test of team effort and real endurance — the 'Log Race'. A team of eight men must carry a log the size of a telegraph pole over a 2.8km course of sand hills in 12-14 minutes. The recruits experience a 'world of pain' in this test designed to simulate pulling a Wombat 120mm recoilless anti-tank gun into action. Letting go of the toggle rope incurs two dreadful penalties: first, the man automatically fails P-Company and, second, he lets his mates down, as they have to struggle to the finish line without him. In the afternoon, the 'Milling' almost provides a few hours of relief as the recruits sit around an impromptu boxing ring waiting to pummel an opponent of roughly the same size and weight for one minute.

On Monday, the selection process starts again as the recruits are faced with completing the classic 16km battle march. Encumbered with a bergen, webbing and personal weapon — total weight nearly 22kg — the squad must run

Left: Soldiers of the US 75th Ranger Regiment receive instruction in hand-to-hand combat and silent killing techniques. All Rangers are highly proficient in unarmed combat skills.

advanced parachute training with the famous 'Pathfinders' of 5 Airborne Brigade.

22 SAS is the world's most famous elite unit. There is no direct entry to the regular SAS, which draws its prospective recruits from the other regiments and corps of the British Army. The process of selection and training lasts almost two years and is designed to weed out all but the most highly motivated. Before embarking on selection, promising candidates are invited to SAS headquarters for a series of introductory films and lectures about the Regiment and its role in the British Army. It was David Stirling's early SAS recruits who started to develop the procedures for British operations behind enemy lines. The basic foundation of the SAS is the four-man patrol, which is small enough to stand the best chance of remaining undetected by the enemy and yet sufficiently skilled and cross-trained to carry the war into the enemy's camp. The SAS man is, of necessity, someone who is self-motivated and able to think for himself. For many applicants, passing into the Regiment will mean

breaking the habits of a lifetime, as the soldiers in most other regiments and corps are conditioned to rely heavily on their officers and noncommissioned officers (NCOs) for orders and direction.

While waiting for a place on winter or summer selection, most serious candidates start to develop their physical fitness and stamina on long road runs. Long solo walks across the Welsh mountains not only hone navigation skills, but also introduce the candidate to hardship and the process of self-reliance, qualities valued by the SAS selection staff.

On their arrival at Stirling Lines in Hereford, the Regiment's home base, the candidates face a short build-up period of road runs and cross-country marches — two weeks for officers and three weeks for enlisted men — before facing the long solo endurance marches of 'final selection'. The men arrive at Test Week physically and mentally exhausted. Ahead of them lie several 30-40km forced marches culminating in the 'Fan Dance' or 'Long Drag' — a 60km forced march over some of the high-

US Marine Corps recruits on the assault course at the Recruit Depot at Parris Island, South Carolina. The Corps believes that only extremely tough training will properly prepare men for battle.

est peaks in the Brecon Beacons, to be completed in around 20 hours carrying a 25kg bergen. The candidates are expected to navigate their way through a series of rendezvous (RV) points that may be no more than a six-figure map reference point on a stark hillside. At each RV the men are checked for signs of exposure or heat stroke, but neither the hot, drying winds of summer nor the cruel blizzards of winter stop the course. Ahead lies an unknown number of RVs and mountain ridges to be crossed. Those with the sheer willpower to keep thinking, while putting one foot in front of the other to keep up the pace, will pass.

The 10 per cent or less who survive the endurance walks are now faced with learning the essential skills for behind-the-lines operations on a 14-week course known as 'Continuation Training'. The physical pressure has eased, but

there are still mental hurdles to be crossed and the candidates can still fail the selection process. Small patrol tactics have to be absorbed and practised until they become second nature. The students learn the contact drills, evasion procedures and arcs of fire that will allow the patrol to survive surprise contact with the enemy. They are taught how to remain unseen and what to carry in their bergen so that they can survive for days, even weeks, in enemy territory.

Personal hygiene and preventive medicine assume a new importance

The signals course introduces the students to the basic principles of covert communications, Morse code and the great variety of radio transmitters employed by the SAS. For many the biggest hurdle will be learning to recognise the sound of high-speed Morse as letters and words, rather than a series of dots and dashes. To pass the course, the men must be able to transmit and receive Morse code at a speed of eight words per minute, which is the standard rate for British Army Regimental Signallers.

A high level of medical skill is also essential for soldiers who operate forward of the usual medical care and evacuation procedures enjoyed by the rest of the army. Personal hygiene and preventive medicine assume a new importance in the decidedly unhealthy environments that the Regiment often finds itself in. From these basics, the students progress to more advanced life-saving techniques usually performed by doctors: setting bones, administering intravenous infusions and recognising and treating a range of infectious diseases.

After a short period of demolitions training, the students find themselves learning the art of combat survival. Lighting fires, snaring game, building survival shelters and staying out of the hands of the enemy prepare the students for the ever-present possibility of being cut off behind enemy lines. A week's survival course in the wilder areas of the British Isles not only provides the opportunity to test these skills, but also softens the men up for a short escape and evasion/resistance to interrogation (RTI) exercise. In common with pilots and other soldiers whose work takes them behind the lines, the prospective SAS troopers must be given every opportunity to avoid capture. If a soldier is taken, he must be able to resist threats, physical and mental brutality and the wiles of his interrogators. The surrendering of any military information, however small, may well lead to the deaths of other patrol members and compromise the entire operation.

A jungle training phase and the static-line parachuting course complete SAS Continuation Training. Even at this late stage applicants can still fail the selection procedure. Entire patrols which have become lost during jungle training have been 'RTU'd' (Returned to Unit), while the parachute course makes further demands on the student's confidence and ability to control fear. Although Selection and Continuation Training are officially over, the trooper now serves a one-year probationary period with one

of the Regiment's operational or 'Sabre' Squadrons. For the 12 months, he will concentrate in depth on one of the essential patrol skills: medicine, demolitions, languages or communications. Equally important are his troop skills. Each 'Sabre' Squadron is divided into four sixteen-man troops, with each one having a speciality: high-altitude, low-opening (HALO) parachuting, small boat/combat swimmer operations, mountain and winter warfare, and long-range vehicle operations. The three-year tour of duty cycle is almost at an end before the SAS soldier has had a chance to learn all the new skills and tasks expected of him. Officers must return to their units at the end of their tour. The enlisted men can opt for a further three years of duty, with the promise of more advanced training in every aspect of their work.

All candidates must be able to swim 50m in boots and clothing

The speciality of the famous American 'Green Berets' is training foreign troops and irregulars in guerrilla and counter-guerrilla (counter-revolutionary) warfare. While they are capable of mounting commando and intelligence gathering operations, these are considered a waste of their special talents and are usually left to the US Army's Rangers. Being accepted for selection for the American Special Forces is almost as tough as passing their infamous course. Most of the enlisted candidates who are accepted for Special Forces selection are sergeants with a minimum of three years service. Officers must wait until their fourth year of service before applying for the Special Forces. All candidates must be able to swim 50m in boots and clothing, pass a general medical and obtain the necessary security clearance. In addition, they must be high school graduates and have passed their advanced physical readiness test, advanced military training and junior NCOs School (E4-E7). Applicants must be airborne qualified and most have successfully completed Ranger School at Fort Benning, if not actually having served with the 75th Ranger Regiment. Not surprisingly, most successful applicants are drawn from the infantry and other combat arms of the Army.

Below: Two students on the US Special Forces Underwater Operations Course come ashore after completing a long-distance qualification swim.

On arrival at the John F. Kennedy Special Warfare Center and School (SWCS), applicants face a tough three-week pre-selection course called Special Forces Assessment and Selection (SFAS). With a traditional failure rate of 25 per cent, SFAS was introduced to make Special Forces selection more cost-effective. Now, three weeks of continuous mental and physical stress persuade the poorly motivated to leave at the beginning of the selection process. Only about half of an average class of 300 candidates pass SFAS and win a place on the Special Forces Qualification Course ('Q' Course).

The course is divided into three phases: common skills, speciality training and a field exercise called 'Robin Sage', where the candidates will be asked to demonstrate all the skills they have learnt on the course. The common skills phase lasts five weeks and concentrates on the basic crafts for a career behind enemy lines. The candidates are taught patrolling, survival, navigation, unarmed combat and airborne insertion and extraction techniques. During the common skills phase, the selectors in the various subject 'committees' watch the candidates, noting not only their ability to absorb this information but watching the student's discipline and self-reliance. Special Forces selection is almost unique in the US Army in that the stu-

Above: Royal Marine Commandos leap ashore from Rigid Raider assault craft. Constant training maintains their high state of battle readiness.

dents are not subjected to any external pressure or pep-talks. Like the SAS, self-motivation is the cornerstone of the training.

At the beginning of week six, the students are divided up into their elected specialities: weapons, communications, engineering or combat medicine. This will be the man's primary skill and function within his 12-man 'A-Team'. Officers have their own training detachment which teaches general operations, intelligence and counter-revolutionary warfare, while acquainting the prospective commanders with all the 'A-Team' specialities. The officers' course has now been re-modelled along the lines of the Australian Special Air Service Regiment's selection course, with an emphasis on field exercises that require the candidates to solve operational problems while under considerable physical and mental stress. There are plans to also extend the Australian philosophy to the rest of the 'Q' Course.

Combat medicine is the longest enlisted man's course, lasts for 21 weeks, and is held at the Academy of Health Sciences at Fort Sam Houston, Texas. There, the students are asked to take a 'mini-medical degree' which covers everything from anatomy and physiology to veterinary medicine and war surgery. Each day begins at 0430 hours and ends long after dark, when the students are given time for private study. The course is so intensive that one commanding officer at the school has commented that most medical students would fail the Green Beret medical course.

Most of the other courses last around 13 weeks. Weapons NCOs receive instruction in all types of foreign weapons, from small arms to anti-tank weapons. On operations the weapons sergeant is responsible for teaching weapons training and small unit tactics to indigenous troops. The engineers learn not only methods of sabotaging railways, bridges and buildings with conventional and home-made explosives, but also learn how to construct bridges, airstrips, roads and fortified emplacements.

Below: Soviet *spetsnaz* have adopted the wolf as their emblem because of its resilience and general ferocity, qualities looked for in recruits.

Covert communications are vital for the re-supply, reinforcement and extraction of Green Beret teams behind enemy lines. To pass the signals course the students must demonstrate a proficiency in antenna design, enciphering and deciphering transmissions, and the principles of 'burst-transmissions' and 'signal-hopping' that are used to avoid enemy radio-location devices. At the end of the course, the students must be able to send and receive Morse code at a minimum speed of eight words per minute.

The exercise simulates a realistic wartime operation

The field exercise is the last phase of selection and is designed to test the skills learnt on the other two phases. The exercise simulates a realistic wartime operation. The students are organised into 'A-Teams' and parachuted into the Uwharrie National Forest. Once inside 'Pinelands', the teams link up with local families who play the role of civilian resistance. Once trained and organised, the 'guerrillas' are

led on a series of raids and ambushes against the 82nd Airborne Division, who play the forces of the 'evil dictator'. Survivors of the 'Q' Course are awarded their green berets and the 'Special Forces' shoulder tabs. As all specialists attached to the Special Forces wear the beret, it is the shoulder tabs that identify the 'Q' Course graduates.

Modern technology has made commando-type raids and other covert operations much more difficult. Sophisticated radar systems, modern fighter, surveillance and AWACs aircraft and air-defence missile systems have made World War II-style static-line parachute drops almost impossible. Equally, the long, lightly defended coastline, once exploited by seaborne raiding forces such as the commandos, can now be covered by comprehensive radar and sonar defence systems. As a consequence, today's raiding parties are delivered by small underwater

Below: Although obviously posed, this unarmed combat shot of *spetsnaz* soldiers amply conveys their aggression and determination.

vehicles or by freefall parachute techniques. While most elite units maintain highly trained cadres for specialist airborne and amphibious warfare operations, the US Navy's Special Warfare Groups (NAVSPECWARGRU) excel in these dangerous roles.

The US Navy deploys two groups. NAVSPECWARGRU ONE is based in Coronado, California, and supports the Pacific Fleet, maintaining a forward deployment unit (Naval Warfare Unit One) for training and support at the Subic Bay complex, Republic of the Philippines. NAVSPECWARGRU TWO is based at Little Creek, Virginia, and is designated the Navy's unconventional warfare planning group for Commander-in-Chief Atlantic Fleet (CINCLANTFLT) and Commander-in-Chief US Naval Forces Europe (CINCUSNAVEUR), maintaining Naval Warfare Unit Two at Roosevelt Road base in Puerto Rico. Each Special Warfare Group consists of three Sea-Air-Land (SEAL) Teams and a Swimmer Delivery Vehicle (SDV) Team (originally Underwater Demolition Teams). These are supported by a Special

Boat Squadron of naval personnel skilled in small boat handling. The last component of the NAVSPECWARGRU is the Inshore Undersea Warfare Groups responsible for protecting American naval installations against attack by enemy special forces.

The American Navy SEALs and the SDV Teams are undoubtedly the most highly trained of the modern US elite forces. Both undergo the same stringent selection process and many naval special forces personnel have served with both units. Applicants for the SEALs must be qualified in a speciality such as medical care, computers and communications, engineering or electronics, have passed a rigorous diving medical, and have produced high scores on physical

and mental aptitude tests. Entry into this elite of elites is by means of the infamous Basic Underwater Demolition/SEAL (BUDS) training programme.

The first four weeks of BUDS is rough by any standard, and every element of the training is competitive as the different teams race against the clock and each other. After a two-week warm-up period, the class learns how to handle different small boats before turning to beach reconnaissance and long-range land patrol skills. Perfection is achieved by the endless repetition of 'live-firing exercises' with the constant pressure to improve accuracy, timing and teamwork. While most of the public think of the SEALs as combat frogmen, the US Navy

Above: *Spetsnaz* **troops practising** *sambo*, **the Russian martial art. Soviet elite units are very rugged; this shot was taken in early February!**

does not share this misconception. As their name implies, these operators are trained to fight in any environment, including far behind enemy lines on land, as recent operations in the 1991 Gulf War demonstrated. This basic phase of selection and training culminates in Motivation, appropriately called 'Hell Week'. More than half of the course have now left in one of two ways, either by being terminated by the course instructors or by ringing a brass bell three times to announce their voluntary withdrawal from BUDS.

Specialist training begins on Week Six with long swims and free-diving exercises to boost confidence. To remain on BUDS, every man must complete a 45m underwater swim and an 8km marathon on the surface. The course then splits into pairs for diving training. The instruction starts with sports scuba equipment but progresses to the LARV-5 Draeger re-breathing rig that eliminates tell-tale bubbles. Recent developments in thermal imaging have made it extremely dangerous to use any equipment that emits bubbles. Swimming in pitch black water, with only a compass to guide them, the students must make a tactical response to all possible diving emergencies. The carbon dioxide scrubber in the rig acts to remove waste products and purify the diver's air, but if the rig floods with sea water the chemicals release a caustic cocktail of gases that burns the man's lungs. If that happens the divers must not only surface, but do so without attracting the attention of an instructor playing the part of an enemy sentry.

The students are also introduced to the array of vehicles that may carry them close to their target. Six nuclear submarines have been converted for SEAL operations including the rather aged *Thomas A. Edison*, the *Thomas Jefferson* and two Polaris boats, the *Sam Houston* and the *John Marshall*. Each of these vessels can carry pods containing SDVs capable of conveying the teams through treacherous tides and currents to the enemy coast. On the surface the craft navigate by computerised satellite and Doppler navigation systems. Once the target is reached, the craft sinks below the harbour defences using sonar to avoid anti-submarine nets and patrol craft. Underwater, the students use a UTEL microphone to communicate with each other and their parent submarine. The device is powered by batteries and has an effective underwater range of 9150m. The sabotage of enemy shipping is now accomplished with a range of light plastic limpet mines and demolition charges but if the target cannot be successfully reached, SDVs such as the EX-IX can lie offshore and fire sophisticated long-range Mark 37 torpedoes.

Leaving an aircraft from an altitude in excess of 10,000m has its drawbacks

After undergoing rigorous specialised underwater warfare training, the students complete a static-line parachute course and learn how to make 'wet' drops into the sea with their equipment. SEAL operations may take the teams inland and far from the coast. Consequently, after qualifying, many SEAL Team members progress to high-altitude, low-opening (HALO) and high-altitude, high-opening (HAHO) parachuting. HALO or military freefall allows the parachutist to descend undetected through the enemy's radar. However, leaving an aircraft from an altitude in excess of 10,000m has its drawbacks. At this height frostbite would occur in minutes and there is so little oxygen that the

parachutist must wear a protective suit and an air/oxygen rig. To this must be added the main and reserve parachutes, an altimeter, weapon and a pack or bergen. Wearing this cumbersome mass of specialist equipment creates great problems with stability. If the parachutist was to start spinning at terminal velocity (190km/hr) the consequences could be disastrous — at best he could hope to pull the ripcord and float down in clear view of the enemy. Most parachutes used by military freefallers are ramair aerofoil section canopies with a glide ratio of 4 to 1 or better, enabling the team to land together with pinpoint accuracy. To avoid the fatalities associated with altimeter failure and human error, the 'chutes are equipped with a barometric opening device designed to deploy the canopy at 600m.

Spetsnaz training methods endeavour to lessen the shock of combat

Another high-altitude parachuting technique which avoids the necessity of aircraft entering enemy air space and can be used where air defences are poor is HAHO — it was reputedly used to insert teams into Kuwait and southern Iraq during Operation 'Desert Storm'. HAHO parachutists leave the aircraft at high altitudes, deploy the 'chute immediately and then glide down onto a chosen landing zone (LZ) 50-60km from the exit point. This is a reasonably simple technique that avoids many of the problems of HALO, though in practice there have been difficulties in actually finding the LZ, particularly during night jumps. This problem has recently been solved with a small chestpack satellite navigation system that guides the parachutist to his LZ.

All post-selection training courses for the US Navy's SEALs are held at the Special Warfare Center and School at Fort Bragg, North Carolina, where the operators are taught most of the subjects found on Special Forces selection. SEAL training is never complete but is deemed satisfactory after the men have completed overseas jungle, desert and arctic warfare training. Such is the 'finishing school' for the men who are asked to handle some of the most dangerous operations in the world.

Above: A glimpse of the special forces of the future? An Israeli female reserve paratrooper.

Another unit which is known for its harsh training is *spetsnaz*, the Soviet Union's special forces. *Spetsnaz* are essentially deep-penetration forces which operate in small groups and fulfil specific roles: neutralisation of nuclear weapons, command centres, air-defence systems, and assassination of key military and political personnel. As these missions are high-risk, *spetsnaz* training methods lessen the shock of combat through realistic simulation.

Assault courses are designed for battle realism and so include flame and water obstacles, jumping between high buildings, and crossing ground which is being raked by live. *Spetsnaz* are trained to a high level in unarmed combat and weapons skills. In common with elite units around the world, *spetsnaz* troops are maintained in a high state of readiness and, as their performance in Afghanistan proved, they do not lack in fighting spirit. *Spetsnaz* are worthy members of the special forces brotherhood.

THE ROYAL MARINES

The Royal Marine Commandos have an illustrious heritage, having fought with honour in World War II, at Suez, in Aden, as well as in the Far East and in the Falklands. Today, they are Britain's elite amphibious spearhead.

THE first British Marine unit was formed on 28 October 1664 at Bunhill Fields in the City of London. Raised as the Duke of York and Albany's Maritime Regiment of Foot, they quickly became known as the Lord High Admiral's Regiment. These 1200 'sea soldiers' were distributed throughout the Royal Navy to provide snipers and to repel enemy boarding parties during the fierce naval engagements of the Second and Third Dutch Wars. Thus began a long association with the Navy, which also found the Marines deployed as landing parties and to maintain discipline on the capital ships of the line. In 1802 their future seemed assured when King George III formally re-named them the Royal Marines (RM). In World War I, Marines served on the Western Front with the Royal Naval Division and took part in the famous raid on the German U-boat base at Zeebrugge (23 April 1918). Despite the fact that the Marines had also adopted the role of naval gunners, at the end of World War I their role had changed little from the one undertaken in the seventeenth century. They were still predominantly 'sea soldiers' and that tradition seemed impregnable.

Firing a GPMG during training in Norway. Constant deployment to the arctic circle to defend NATO's northern flank has meant that the Corps now has great expertise in arctic warfare.

The transition to amphibious operations began in the early 1920s when the Royal Marine Light Infantry and RM Artillery were combined into a single corps. The corps was then subdivided to form the Mobile Naval Base Defence Organisation, charged with seizing and defending naval anchorages, and the Royal Marines Division, deployed in support of landings and other various operations ashore. The balance, less than a third of the corps, remained with the naval gunnery detachments. In 1942, the Royal Marine Commandos were raised to serve alongside the 11 Army Commandos in four elite Special Service (Commando) Brigades under the overall control of the Director of Combined Operations.

One of the first to see any action was 40 (RM) Commando, when it joined Nos 3 and 4 Commandos and the American Rangers on the bloody beaches of Dieppe in August 1942. The attack on the small coastal resort was by way of a rehearsal for the D-Day landings and also acted as a sop to the Soviets, who were insisting that the Allies open a second front in Europe. Surprise was lost early in the operation and the main beaches quickly became a killing ground for successive waves of Canadian infantry. The

Below: Members of 40 Commando at Lake Comacchio in April 1945. The battles to take key positions resulted in heavy commando casualties.

commandos attacked coastal batteries on the flanks of the main force. Although there were heavy casualties amongst the infantry, the commando operations enjoyed reasonable success and both commandos and airborne forces were later used to secure and extend the flanks of the Normandy invasion beaches in June 1944.

Throughout the campaign the brigade was used as line infantry

After the Dieppe raid, 40 Commando joined 43 Commando and Nos 2, 9, and 10 Commandos in the 2nd Special Service (Commando) Brigade for operations in Italy. Throughout the campaign the brigade was used as line infantry, incurring very heavy casualties while assaulting strongpoints in the Appenine Mountains. In April 1943, the commandos were returned to a more unconventional role: supporting Tito's Yugoslavian partisans in the Dalmatian Islands. Towards the end of the war, the Brigade returned to Italy, joining other commando and Special Air Service (SAS) units for the assault across the Comacchio lagoon in April 1945.

The 3rd Special Service (Commando) Brigade was formed in November 1943 from Nos 1, 5, 42 (RM) and 44 (RM) Commandos for operations in the Far East. The brigade saw action as the Allies finally retook Burma, taking part in the amphibious landings in the Arakan and

supporting the main assault on Mandalay. The two other Special Service Brigades were formed to support the invasion of Europe. The 1st Special Service (Commando) Brigade was raised by Brigadier Lord Lovat and consisted of Nos 3, 4, 6 and 45 (RM) Commandos, while the 4th SS (Cdo) Bde was entirely Royal Marine — composed of four Commandos (Nos 41, 46, 47 and 48) under the command of a Royal Marine, Brigadier B. W. Leicester.

The perimeter was already under attack by the 21st Panzer Division

The job of the commandos on D-Day was to help breach the German Atlantic Wall, a series of heavily fortified villages and coastal resorts surrounded by minefields and defended in force by artillery and infantry. It was suicidal to commit lightly armed commandos against such formidable defensive positions. Consequently, the very first troops to land were line infantry supported by tanks and specialised armoured vehicles tasked with smashing through the obstacle belts and securing a beachhead. The commandos landed 90 minutes later to subdue the numerous strongpoints and extend the beachheads forward and laterally, linking up the Anglo-Canadian forces on the beaches and reinforcing the 6th Airborne Division.

Lovat's commandos landed on 'Sword' Beach, taking their initial objectives but leaving the heavily fortified gun positions inside the Ouistreham casino to the French commandos. At midday, the commandos arrived at Pegasus Bridge over the Caen Canal. To the south, the perimeter was already under attack by elements of the 21st Panzer Division, which was attempting to break through to the invasion beaches. Towards the coast, the Merville Battery, stormed by paratroopers assault in the early hours of the morning, was back in action and bombarding 'Sword' Beach. Farther north, the roads and coastal towns of Franceville Plage and Cabourg were still held by the Germans. Leaving a force at the bridge, Lovat's men moved towards their objectives. As evening approached, they were treated to the welcome sight of 6th Air Landing Brigade's glider reinforcements crossing the French coast.

Above: Soldiers from 41 Commando prepare to blow up a strategically important North Korean railway line during the Korean War (1950-53).

Over the next two days, the commandos pushed north towards the coast. While two troops of No 3 Commando were despatched to silence the battery, the Royal Marines of 45 Commando cleared Sallenelles and Merville before engaging German troops in Franceville Plage. On the outskirts of the town, the Royal Marines discarded their rucksacks and fought their way to the beach, garden by garden. Under a relentless German counterattack, the Royal Marines' positions in Franceville Plage became untenable. Behind them the town of Sallenelles had changed hands several times in the vicious hand-to-hand fighting. More than half of 45 Commando were dead, missing or wounded. Around midnight on 8 June, the Royal Marines withdrew to the British positions at Merville. Some of the commandos, exhausted by three days of continuous fighting, fell asleep and were killed by the Germans when they recaptured the town.

Above: Royal Marines conducting house-to-house searches in Port Said during Operation 'Musketeer', the Anglo-French invasion of Egypt.

Across the British-Canadian beaches, the other RM Commandos had suffered similar casualties. 41 Commando braved heavy fire on 'Sword' Beach to assault Lion-sur-Mer before attacking the Douvres radar station. Both 48 and 46 Commandos landed on 'Juno' Beach, where 48 Commando lost half of its force on the shingle opposite surviving concrete strongpoints in the resort of St Aubin. Undeterred, they marched east to assault the equally murderous coastal defences situated at Langrune. Landing a day later, 46 Commando moved south to successfully secure the Mue River valley and evict the Waffen SS of the 12th *Hitler Jugend* Division from the villages of Le Hamel and Rots. Finally, 47 Commando landed on 'Gold' Beach to take the fishing village of Port-en-Bessin from the rear. Situated between

'Omaha' and 'Gold' Beaches, the heavily defended port was to be the final destination of the Allied cross-Channel petrol line 'Pluto' (Pipe Line Under The Ocean).

Over the next crucial months, as the Allied armies prepared for the break out, the left flank continued to be held by the two commando brigades and the paratroops. On 17 August, as the Allies thrust east towards the River Seine, the red and green berets continued to guard the left flank of the Canadian First Army. As the Germans withdrew, blowing river and canal bridges behind them, the paras and commandos remained in contact. Under heavy shelling, the

Above: A four-man squad from 42 Commando on patrol near the Indonesian border, in the Sabah region of the Federation of Malaysia, in 1965.

3rd Para Brigade forced a crossing of a deep canal and advanced into Pont l'Eveque, engulfed in such an intense blaze that tanks were catching fire in the streets. Fighting their way through the outskirts of the town, the paras were able to secure a crossing over the River Touques, aided by the two commando brigades which launched a flanking attack to envelop the retreating Germans. In the words of paratroop commander, Major-General Gale, '...the green and red berets have fought as one.'

The Royal Marines of the 4th SS Brigade saw another bitterly contested landing when they fought their way into Walcheren in September 1944 to help clear the mouth of the Scheldt and free the port of Antwerp for Allied shipping. After Walcheren was taken, the Brigade continued to harry the Germans on the islands in the Mass/Rhine estuaries. Meanwhile, the 1st SS Brigade, which included 45 and 46 (RM) Commandos, was used to breach the Siegfried Line at several points, joining the 6th Airborne Division once again for the attack on Osnabruck and the crossing of the River Weser in April 1945.

In the years following World War II the Royal Marines were involved in numerous actions outside of Europe. In 1956, 40, 42 and 45 Commandos took part in Operation 'Musketeer', the Anglo-French intervention in Egypt following the latter's nationalisation of the Suez Canal. 40 and 42 Commandos conducted an amphibious assault on Port Said on 6 November, while 45 made one of the first recorded helicopter assault operations when they landed in the city on the same day. During the next few days the commandos, together with paras, Centurion tanks of the Royal Tank Regiment and aircraft of the Fleet Air Arm, and supported by naval gunfire, began to clear Port Said of Egyptian troops. The Royal Marines were heavily involved in the unpleasant business of house-clearing, which cost them a total of nine dead and 60 wounded.

The commandos had to call on all their reserves of stamina and fortitude

From April 1960 to November 1967 Royal Marines served in the town and colony of Aden. The commandos had to call on all their reserves of stamina and fortitude in their battles against the forces of the National Liberation Front (NLF), the Front for the Liberation of

South Yemen (FLOSY) and the South Arabian League. The British launched numerous operations against rebel areas which involved Royal Marine units, a notable one being Operation 'Cut' in 1965. In this mission men from 45 Commando assaulted an enemy-held position in the inhospitable Radfan region, approximately 10km east of Dhala. The action was no different to countless others that were conducted in that unforgiving terrain: after a long approach in the blistering heat the Marines would launch their attack supported by air strikes, after which the position would be taken, only to be abandoned after a short occupation.

The Marines' superior weapons skills brought them many victories

The war against an elusive foe was unrelenting; during a two-month period in 1965, for example, 45 Commando conducted no less than 305 major patrols in the Radfan area alone. Towards the end of British rule in the colony, 45 Commando was also deployed in a peacekeeping role in the port of Aden itself. The rabbit warren-like streets of the town provided an ideal environment for snipers and grenade attacks. The British presence, together with the Marines, including, briefly, 42 Commando, left the port for good on 29 November 1967.

Royal Marines were also engaged in the Far East, where the were involved in the defence of the recently-formed Federation of Malaysia against a belligerent Indonesia. Both 40 and 42 Commandos took part in the fighting, which occurred predominantly in the southwestern Sarawak region. Between 1962 and 1966 the Marines undertook a wide variety of operations among the swamps, rivers and waterways, conducting firefights, ambushes and cross-border raids. The Marines' superior training and weapons skills brought them many victories. In one particular incident in August 1963, a large force of guerrillas and Indonesian troops attacked a border post manned by one company from 42 Commando and a section of locally-raised Border Scouts. Despite repeated attacks over three nights' the position held, and on the fourth night the garrison launched its own sortie, which forced the enemy back over the border.

Above: A mortar team from 45 Commando dug in on Mount Kent, East Falkland, in June 1982. During the whole of the campaign the Royal Marines lost 27 men killed and 67 wounded.

Operating in a jungle environment severely tested the Marines' concentration, where long periods of patrolling and surveillance would be followed by short, violent contacts with the enemy at short ranges. However, by early 1966 the resilience of the British, Malaysian and Commonwealth troops began to dishearten the Indonesian people. Their president, Sukarno, who had engineered the 'Confrontation', was overthrown in March of that year. Five months later, Indonesia made peace with Malaysia, bringing the campaign to an end.

Since the start of the 'Troubles' in 1969, Royal Marines have also patrolled the violent

streets of Ulster, making their contribution in the fight against terrorism in this seemingly endless war. In April 1982, a major conflict developed in the South Atlantic when Argentinian forces invaded the British Falkland Islands and claimed them as Argentine territory. The Royal Marines were duly summoned to spearhead the task force despatched to re-establish British sovereignty.

The assault began with X Company moving forward to capture a ridge

The advance to the capital, Stanley, was spearheaded by 3 Para and 45 Commando, after the successful British landings at San Carlos on 21 May. Ahead lay a series of Argentine mountain-top positions held by approximately 8-9000 conscripts in often superb defensive positions.

Phase one of the battle to clear these positions began on the night of the 11/12 June, with a three-pronged brigade attack to take Mounts Longdon, Harriet and the twin peaks of Two Sisters. The assault began with 3 Para's attack on Mount Longdon, which was taken at a cost of 18 soldiers, one of whom, Sergeant McKay, was awarded the Parachute Regiment's second posthumous Victoria Cross of the campaign.

As the battle for Longdon raged, 45 Commando, in the centre, moved towards their start-lines for the attack on Two Sisters. The assault began with X Company moving forward to capture a ridge, nicknamed 'Long Toenail', from which they could lay down suppressive fire in support of the main advance from the northwest and cover Goat Ridge on the perimeter of 42 Commando's assault on Mount Harriet. However, X Company's attack was seriously delayed by the rough going and the weight of the equipment and support weapons. The first pinnacle of 'Toenail' was gained quickly, but then X Company ran into heavy machine-gun fire which pinned down 1 and 3 Troop's overall advance along the ridge. When 2 Troop finally gained the summit they were immediately shelled by Argentine artillery.

The delay was used to good effect by Y and Z Companies, which moved out of the Murrell Bridge area and slowly made their way forward to the Argentinian positions, first missing an enemy artillery barrage that fell across the line of advance. However, soon after midnight the two companies were illuminated by moonlight and a furious firefight developed 300m from the Argentine positions. A pre-planned artillery strike battered the enemy trenches and allowed Z Company to overwhelm the enemy positions in hand-to-hand fighting. On the right, and under heavy mortar and .50 calibre machine-gun fire, Y Company advanced between the two peaks, clearing the high ground along the ridge line. The Two Sisters were finally captured after a two-and-a-half-hour battle at a loss of four Royal Marines killed and 11 wounded.

Below: Two members of the Special Boat Service paddle a wooden-framed Klepper canoe.

Right: A heavily camouflaged Royal Marine 'yomps' across open terrain. Stamina building forms a large part of Royal Marines' training.

To the south, Mount Harriet proved to be more formidable, being surrounded to the west and south by a sea of minefields. The Brigade's last target for the night was allotted to 42 Commando. The skilful use of reconnaissance patrols by the unit's commander, Lieutenant-Colonel Nick Vaux, had produced a relatively mine-free route for a long encircling advance to take Harriet from the rear. Diversionary artillery fire falling on the western slopes of Mount Harriet was intended to persuade the enemy that the commandos planned a suicidal frontal attack across the 900m of heavily mined open ground to the west. The ploy worked, as L and K Companies were already amongst the Argentinian defenders before the alarm was raised. As snipers and heavy machine gun posts were eliminated by Milan anti-tank missiles, the commandos swarmed up the slopes to clear the trenches. The battle, fought at a cost of two dead and 20 wounded, netted 300 prisoners and was later hailed by Brigadier Julian Thompson, 3 Commando Brigade's commander, as 'a really crafty, cunning attack, with all the Commando elements — quite brilliant.'

The Royal Marines are commanded by the Commandant-General Royal Marines, through Headquarters Commando Forces, which organises the operations and exercises for UK-based commandos and is responsible for the deployment of the whole of 3 Commando Brigade. The latter remains committed to the defence of NATO's northern flank in Norway and to providing 'out of area' forces in the British national interest or relief and peacekeeping forces under British or United Nations command. Based at Arbroath in Scotland, 45 Commando was the first unit to specialise in cold weather warfare, carrying out regular exercises in Norway. In the 1970s they were joined by 42 Commando, forming the core of a British ski-borne force trained in mountain and arctic warfare and tasked with defending NATO's northern front. The First Amphibious Combat Group and 'Whiskey Company', Royal Netherlands Marine Corps, also come under the overall command of 3 Commando Brigade. In the event of hostilities in Norway, the British will be joined by the ACE Mobile Force, a US Marine Amphibious Brigade and the Canadian Air-Sea Transportable (CAST) Brigade Group. In contrast, the major role of 40 Commando is 'out of area' operations, and so it trains regularly in the jungles of Brunei and takes part in annual NATO amphibious exercises held in Europe and the Caribbean.

Above: A Sea King helicopter prepares to recover a Rigid Raider and its crew. These craft are used by 539 Assault Squadron based at Plymouth.

The House was stormed with anti-tank missiles and small-arms fire

The Royal Marines maintain a number of sub-units for special missions. Comacchio Group is based with 45 Commando at Arbroath and tasked with internal security duties. One half of the Group is responsible for the security of naval bases and Britain's nuclear arsenal, while the other half specialises in the protection of oil rigs. Most of these highly trained Marines are graduates of the close personal protection and close quarter battle courses, which are run by the Marine's counter-terrorist school at Poole in Dorset.

The Mountain and Arctic Warfare Cadre (M&AWC) was formed from the Cliff Assault Wing to teach the commandos arctic warfare and provide instruction in cliff and mountain climbing to the men of the more specialised Reconnaissance Troops. In times of war the M&AWC is trained to carry out various long-range reconnaissance patrols and deep raiding tasks for HQ Commando Forces. Trained to survive the unfriendly environment of the Norwegian wilderness in winter, the Cadre excelled in the Falkland Islands. When hostilities broke out the Cadre was actually running a Mountain Leaders (ML2) course, and the instructors and their students formed the basis of an operational detachment that was able to travel south with 3 Commando Brigade.

Within a week of the landings, a high profile operation brought the unit deserved fame. As 3 Para and 45 Commando left the beachhead, reconnaissance teams and patrols were deployed far forward to observe and harass the enemy. When Argentine Special Forces were found to be occupying Top Malo House, close to one of the British objectives at Teal Inlet, 20 members of the Cadre were lifted forward to eject them. On 31 May, they fought the only daylight action of the war when the House was stormed with anti-tank missiles and small-arms fire. Five enemy soldiers were killed and another 12 captured as they fled the burning house.

The other highly specialised unit deployed by the Royal Marines is their Special Boat Squadron (SBS), now renamed the Special Boat Service. Today's SBS operator is a highly trained swimmer/canoeist and parachutist capable of performing a variety of missions. In the South Atlantic in 1982, 2 SBS were involved in the re-capture of South Georgia and 6 SBS provided some of the first reconnaissance teams to land on East Falkland. After placing reconnaissance/surveillance patrols to cover the landings at San Carlos, SBS teams took part in the preparation to the raid on Pebble Island air base, and even managed to infiltrate the old wreck of the *Lady Elizabeth* in Stanley Harbour. From their cold, damp vantage point, the patrol

Below: Safeguarding the Kurds — Royal Marines operating in northern Iraq in May 1991.

reported back that the garrison's officers congregated every night in the post office. At first light on 11 June, a Wessex helicopter approached and fired two AS-12 missiles at the requisitioned officer's mess. Fired from 4570m out, one missile went into the sea, while the other struck the police station across the road.

Another specialist unit was raised during the Falklands conflict to provide small boat amphibious capability. The Task Force Landing Craft Squadron brought together elements of the Landing Craft Branch and the 1st Raiding Squadron, which were both amphibious support units. On the Royal Marines' return to Britain this became 539 Assault Squadron (RM). At present, it consists of four Troops: Raiding Troop with three sections equipped with five Rigid Raiders; Landing Craft Troop with two Landing Craft Utility (LCUs), four landing Craft Vehicle Personnel (LCVPs) and an Assault Beach Unit (ABU); Support Troop, which provides mechanical and engineering support; and Headquarters Troop.

All commando-trained personnel sport the green beret. The army and support units wear their own cap badge, while the Royal Marines beret badge is the 'Great Globe' encircled with laurel and bearing the motto *Per Mare, Per Terram* — By Sea, By Land.

THE US MARINE CORPS & NAVY SEALS

The US Marine Corps is a massive, self-contained amphibious strike force. Equipped with ships, vehicles and aircraft, it can project American power around the world.

SINCE its formation by Act of Congress in 1775, the United States Marine Corps (USMC) has always been the first choice to protect American interests throughout the world. Originally formed to provide naval vessels with snipers and boarding parties, its tasks expanded to include the protection of the many US shore bases guarding vital trade links with Africa and the Far East. Although in theory a part of the Department of the Navy, the Marines are in fact an independent force and their Commandant is a member of the Joint Chiefs of Staff.

The USMC is the largest elite unit in the world and, arguably, one of the earliest rapid deployment forces to see service. In 1931, Secretary of War Patrick J. Hurley outlined the Marines' very special position within American foreign policy: 'The Marine Corps can land on foreign

US Marines in Saudi Arabia during the 1991 Gulf War. When Iraq invaded Kuwait in August 1990 it was the Marines who were among the first foreign troops to be sent to the Gulf.

41

territory without it being considered an act of war, but when the Army moves on foreign territory that is an act of war and that is one of the reasons for the Corps.' Not surprisingly, the Marines became known on Capitol Hill as the 'State Department's Troops'.

And, of course, in battle they had proved their commitment and worth. During World War I, for example, over 13,000 Marines were killed or wounded in the trenches. Between the wars, Marine battalions were sent to defend the Pacific islands. Small detachments were in place on these islands when Japanese bombers attacked the US Pacific Fleet at Pearl Harbor on 7 December 1941. The subsequent Japanese offensive in the southwest Pacific captured most of New Guinea and part of the Solomon Islands. America had been taken by surprise. When a Japanese task force arrived off the coast of Guam, a mere 130 Marines were available to defend the island. In retreat, the Corps adopted the Commando/Ranger philosophy and formed Marine Raider battalions (1st-4th) and two Raider Regiments. As the tide of war turned these special units, with the 1st and 2nd Marine Divisions, were asked to capture the Pacific islands and, in doing so, fought in some of the bloodiest battles of World War II.

The Japanese landed first, occupying the island with a small force

The massive war machines of America and Japan clashed over control of the Solomon Islands. Central to the battle for the Solomons was the island of Guadalcanal — a 145km long, 40km wide tropical paradise. The Japanese forces landed first, occupying the island with a small force and building a vital airstrip, as this long chain of islands was at the maximum range of Japanese land-based aircraft. Consequently, Japan's invasion was initially supplied and reinforced by sea, using a long, vulnerable sea lane called 'The Slot' that ran through the centre of the island group. Guadalcanal and its airstrip began to assume a major strategic importance to both sides.

Between the 7th and 14th of August 1942, the Americans launched a powerful counter-invasion with landings on Guadalcanal and nearby Tulagi. By 21 August, Lunga airfield was captured, re-named Henderson Field, and brought into service with the support of a US carrier force to the south of Guadalcanal. The Japanese now had no option but to continue reinforcing their troops on Guadalcanal by sea, prompting US warships and aircraft to move to intercept them. In the six subsequent naval battles the Americans lost two cruisers and six destroyers sunk, while the Japanese lost two battleships, two cruisers, three destroyers and 11 transport ships.

Successive companies of Japanese troops rolled over the cordon

The fighting on the island, expected to last a week at most, developed into a vicious struggle that continued into February 1943. The Marine Divisions, Paramarines (Marine parachute companies) and the Raiders, who had all taken part in the initial landings, continued to cling to the small beachhead around Henderson Field. In early September, as the Japanese massed to overrun the airfield, the Marines prepared a pre-emptive strike. Three companies of the 1st Raider Battalion and several Paramarine companies landed at Tasimboko and swung west to move against the flank and rear of the 4000-strong Kawaguchi force. Caught by surprise, the Japanese withdrew and the Marines fanned out to extend the defensive perimeter. Two nights later, three battalions of Major-General Kawaguchi's brigade counter-attacked, breaking on the American trenches like waves on a beach. Successive companies of Japanese troops rolled over the defensive cordon in 10 hours of savage hand-to-hand fighting. The Marines were pushed back to a perimeter so tight that the shells from their 105mm howitzers were almost falling back on the gun crews. Enemy troops who broke through the Marines' cordon were ruthlessly eliminated in vicious close quarter combat. At dawn the fighting slowed as the Japanese survivors withdrew, leaving the airfield firmly in American hands.

Guadalcanal became a savage patrol war as the Americans began to strengthen their grip on the island. One long-range patrol became famous not only for the damage it inflicted on

Men of the 2nd Marine Division in action on Saipan in July 1944. The Japanese often had to be flushed out with flamethrowers and grenades.

the enemy, but also for the time spent behind enemy lines. On 4 November, elements of the 147th Infantry Regiment and the 5th Defense Regiment seized a second beachhead at Aolo, allowing the 2nd Raiders to move into the jungle for a 240km patrol back to the US positions at Henderson Field. For the next month the Raiders fought a running battle with the 228th Infantry Regiment, killing an estimated 175 Japanese for the loss of only six Marines. The Americans cut a large swathe through the Japanese lines of communications. More importantly, the patrol culminated in a series of raids that destroyed the Japanese artillery which had been shelling Henderson Field. In the wake of such actions, the Japanese high command decided that Guadalcanal was a lost position and withdrew its 10,652-strong garrison over three nights between the 2nd and 8th of February 1943. The ground and naval battles, including the loss of troops in transports, had cost Japan some 20,000 soldiers and 860 aircraft, in addition to 24 naval vessels sunk.

So the Marines pushed on, taking the defences with grim determination

The US Marines' experiences of war in the southwest Pacific helped formulate the present philosophy of using well-supported, overwhelming force during amphibious landings. In the battles for the islands than ran across the Pacific to the coast of Japan itself, the Marines needed overwhelming force. The island chains offered America secure bases from which to launch the final attack on the Japanese mainland. Each island brought the Americans closer to Tokyo Bay, but the Japanese never evacuated a major garrison again. After Guadalcanal the Japanese attempted to wipe out the Americans with massed-wave attacks. After Saipan was taken (6 July 1944), Japanese tactics changed

Below: Marines pour ashore from landing craft in the first assault wave at Inchon, September 1950.

again. At Guam, Tinian, Leyte, Iwo Jima and Okinawa the Japanese fought from carefully constructed fortifications.

Landings by the US Marines and infantry were preceded by intensive naval and air bombardment. Rows of battleships and hundreds of US aircraft battered the defences mercilessly, decapitating trees and smashing coral into pieces of deadly shrapnel that increased the fragmentation effect of the bombs and shells. Below ground, the Japanese waited patiently in tunnels and bunkers cut deep into the coral. As the bombardment lifted, the defenders swarmed into their trenches and started to lay down a murderous rain of interlocking mortar and machine-gun fire. Meanwhile, landing craft left the protective screen around the assault ships and began their perilous journey towards the beach. At Tarawa (November 1943) the surrounding coral reef forced the Marines to wade through shallow water for hundreds of metres while under intense fire. On Hollandia (April 1944) they had to negotiate tidal mangrove swamps that threatened to hold them fast in clinging mud.

Above: A typical scene from the Vietnam War. A 'Huey' takes off after delivering supplies to a Marine position 'somewhere in the Nam'.

Once on the beach, it was difficult to dig foxholes in the thin layer of volcanic ash, mud or sand that covered the coral skeleton of the islands. So the Marines pushed on, taking the defences with grim determination. As eight-man squads closed on a trench or a bunker, two men on the flanks would rush forward and throw grenades into the pit. After the other entrances and exits had been found and grenaded, the tunnels were cleared with bayonets, grenades and machine guns. Subsequent assault waves brought in the Marine and Army M4 Sherman tanks, which provided some cover as they eliminated the bunkers with 75mm shells, grenades or flamethrowers. All too frequently, the Japanese retreated into a tunnel complex to reappear again behind the Marines in trenches thought to have been cleared. The jungle also hid a large number of enemy snipers, who waited for the first wave of Americans to pass them by before opening fire — a deadly foe who was only revealed by flamethrowers or by shredding the trees with heavy machine-gun fire. At night the Americans listened for the tell-tale sounds of infiltrators or enemy companies forming for a suicidal counterattack,

while hoping to catch some sleep before the bloody business began again at dawn.

Iwo Jima (February-May 1945) was bought with blood and the lives of 6800 Marines and 900 sailors, with another 20,000 being wounded. In addition, another 2000 naval personnel were listed as wounded or missing. When the fighting was finally over, the island was covered with over 20,000 Japanese dead. The next stop was Okinawa — an island fortress in the Ryukyu chain held by an army of 130,000 Japanese troops concealed in many interlocking bunker and trench systems. The Japanese home islands were only 800km to the north and, though the garrison was not expected to surrender, nothing prepared the Americans for the nightmare that was to come.

Artillery and tanks dug into the mountain ridges were used to deadly effect

Following a massive naval bombardment, American forces landed on 1 April 1945. The landing was unopposed and at first it seemed as though the barrage had broken the enemy's morale. It was only when the defenders poured out of the tunnels that it became obvious that the Americans were facing what amounted to a huge ambush. Light artillery and tanks dug into the mountain ridges were used to deadly effect.

45

The overall US commander, General Buckner, was killed when a concealed battery of deadly 47mm rapid-fire anti-tank guns opened up on his headquarters group. Buckner and his officers were engulfed by deadly coral slivers thrown up by the bursting shells. At Kunishi Ridge, the 7th Marine Regiment found itself facing defenders hidden deep inside the ridge itself. It was destroyed section by section. The heavily defended entrances and bunkers were pounded by tanks and finally cleared by infantry assaults. Then the entrances and tunnels linking the bunkers and trenches were sealed with explosives, entombing the defenders alive — an estimated 20,000 died in this manner.

On Okinawa itself, 100,000 Japanese were killed as whole units fought to the last man. The savage battle continued until 21 June, with another 9000 Japanese being killed in mopping-up operations. Only 10,000 local troops chose to surrender to the Americans, who also suffered heavy losses — the three regiments of the 1st Marine Division, for example, lost over 7500 men. As veterans were killed or wounded, replacements were rushed forward. If the latter were killed before documentation they were simply listed as 'Missing'. Some units lost one and a half times their entire complement.

The Marines also saw extensive service in the Korean War (1950-1953), most notably at Inchon in September 1950. The amphibious landings conducted by the 1st Marine Division on the 15th was the brainchild of General Douglas MacArthur, who planned to halt the Communist offensive which was threatening to overrun the whole of the Korean peninsula. Just before dawn on 15 September, 20,000 Marines prepared to storm ashore. MacArthur's daring plan caught the enemy unawares and, by the evening of 16 September, Inchon was secure after very light resistance. Three days later, the Marines had captured Kimpo airport, only 15km west of Seoul.

North Korean units now began to organise themselves, launching a series of counterattacks to regain control of Seoul. In one particular

Left: A CH-46 Sea Knight lifts off from a hill post at Khe Sanh. The siege cost the Marines 199 dead and 830 wounded. NVA losses are put at 15,000.

incident, on 26 September, a large force of North Korean tanks and self-propelled guns attacked the positions of the 1st Marine Regiment. Despite a ferocious enemy onslaught the Marines halted the attack, destroying seven tanks and killing over 500 enemy personnel. By 29 September the North Koreans were in full retreat and the whole area was secure. Though Inchon was the most spectacular action the Marines were involved in, the Corps continued to give sterling service in Korea until the signing of the armistice in July 1953.

The Marines were caught in a hail of small-arms and mortar fire

Some 12 years later they were again involved in a war in the Far East: Vietnam. The Corps' lengthy involvement in the conflict began in 1962 when 24 UH-34D military helicopters were deployed in support of the South Vietnamese armed forces. In February 1965, the decision was taken to commit ground troops to Vietnam and elements of the 3rd Marine Division landed at Da Nang in March. By August four Marine Regiments and four Marine Air Groups were in Vietnam. More Marine units arrived throughout 1965 and 1966, one of them being the 26th Marines, which was sent to protect an important airfield in a remote northwestern valley called Khe Sanh. This was part of General Westmoreland's plan, commander of the US Military Assistance Command, Vietnam (MACV), to tighten the grip on the five northernmost provinces of Vietnam. Designed to be a small military 'dagger' pointing at the communist supply lines along the long Laotian border, Khe Sanh soon became a logistical vortex that sucked in both men and equipment including a large helicopter force and US Army 175mm batteries to provide artillery support.

On 24 April 1967, a five-man forward observer party was ambushed on Hill 861. For the next three days, two Marine companies attempted to clear the hill, only to discover that the North Vietnamese Army (NVA) 325C Division had occupied 861 and two adjoining ridges — Hills 881 South and 881 North. Within metres of the communist defences, the Marines were caught in a hail of small-arms and mortar fire.

Despite artillery support and the ever-present helicopter gunships and jets of the 1st Marine Aircraft Wing, the NVA remained in contact as the Marines carried away their dead and wounded. When the hill was finally retaken, Lieutenant-General Lew Walt saw something he had not seen since the war in the Pacific. The hill had been turned into a huge fortress with 400 foxholes and 25 bunkers interlinked by tunnels. The bunkers themselves, covered with two metres of bamboo and packed earth, were designed to withstand a direct hit from anything but the largest munitions. The hills had become a deadly ambush; the farther up the hill the Marines advanced the worse it became. On Hill 881 South, the Marines discovered an underground fortress 10 times the size of that on the northern ridge. Walt duly ordered his Marines withdrawn from the hills and requested air strikes with 1000 and 2000lb bombs equipped with delayed fuzes. It was hoped that the massive subterranean shock waves would collapse the underground fortifications. Finally, engineers surrounded the base with a cordon of seismic detectors which were wired into fire support. The battles for the hills had cost the lives of 155 Marines; another 425 wounded had been evacuated.

Mortar rounds, 122mm rockets and shells were pounding the air base

At the end of 1967, all the intelligence indicators suggested that the communists were planning a climactic battle. Westmoreland believed it would occur at Khe Sanh. As if to prove him right, 20,000 NVA soldiers and a regiment of artillery moved back into the hills overlooking the air base. One of the units was the 304th Division. Its battle pennants were emblazoned with the name of a communist victory that had finally defeated the French under circumstances and in terrain similar to the Khe Sanh valley: Dien Bien Phu in March 1954. By this time the garrison numbered 6000 men including Marines, South Vietnamese Rangers and other support units. On the night of 20 January, the Marines' hill outposts came under attack. By morning, mortar rounds, 122mm rockets and shells were pounding the

air base, while secondary explosions shook the defenders as ammunition dumps were hit. Burning shells cartwheeled across the base, exploding on impact. Tear gas from the burning arsenal added to the general confusion.

It was the start of a siege that would last 77 days until the beginning of April, but it was only a part of a much larger offensive throughout the whole of South Vietnam. In the early hours of 31 January, as the world watched events unfolding at Khe Sanh, 15 Viet Cong (VC) battalions attacked towns and cities across South Vietnam — the Tet Offensive had begun. The Americans and their allies were caught woefully unprepared, as the communists had declared a seven-day cease-fire during the holiday period. With the 1st Marine Division spread thinly across the I Corps Zone and reinforcements standing by to relieve Khe Sanh, the strategic city of Hue was retaken by two battalions of Marines and supporting Army of the Republic of Vietnam (ARVN) units in some of the worst fighting of the war.

These low-intensity wars required a different sort of military response

The Marines stayed in Vietnam to the end. During the gradual withdrawal of US forces, beginning in 1969, Marine units replaced outgoing Army battalions. By September 1970 the 5th and 7th Marines had been withdrawn, the 3rd Amphibious Force had been replaced by an Amphibious Brigade and only three regiments of the 1st Marine Division remained. In July 1971, the Marine contingent inside the country was reduced to Embassy guards and advisors but the Corps would briefly return. In 1975, an Amphibious Ready Group lay off the coast of Cambodia for 44 days before it evacuated US citizens from Phnom Penh. Later the same force became part of the Marine Brigade that helped evacuate Saigon. US Marines also played a central role in the last American combat operation of the war in Southeast Asia — the rescue of the USS *Mayaguez* and its crew from the Khmer Rouge.

During the 1980s, the Marines' role changed significantly as a consequence of the changing nature of conflict around the world.

The threat of large-scale conventional and nuclear war between America and the Soviet Union receded, but the spectre of low-intensity conflicts grew larger, partly as a consequence of the lessening of Superpower rivalry. These low-intensity wars required a different sort of military response. In addition, a changing role was also prompted by the decline in the numbers of US foreign naval bases, which fell from 450 in 1947 to a mere 120 in the 1980s.

These changes might have spelt the end for the Marines, however the Corps adapted, tailoring integrated Marine Air-Ground Task Forces (MAGTF) for specific military missions. Immediate emergencies are usually handled by forward-deployed Marine Expeditionary Units (MEU), each consisting of a reinforced infantry battalion, a helicopter squadron and supporting

Below: A USMC Light Armoured Vehicle (LAV) during Operation 'Just Cause' in December 1989. The Corps has a total of 416 in its inventory.

arms within a fast amphibious task force. Two MEUs are currently maintained, one in the Mediterranean and one in the Western Pacific.

If a larger force is required, MEUs can be organised into a Marine Expeditionary Brigade (MEB), which is itself the forward echelon of the parent Marine Expeditionary Force (MEF). There are currently three MEFs, two under the US Pacific Command and one under the US Atlantic Command. Each MEF comprises helicopters and fixed-wing aircraft of the Marine Aircraft Wing, combat troops and supporting arms (Marine Division) and a Force Service Support Group of engineer and transport assets — in total 50,800 Marines, 2600 sailors and the necessary advanced military technology to make opposed landings: 70 tanks, 200 armoured personnel carriers (APCs), 120 artillery pieces, 156 combat aircraft and 24 armed helicopters. The Corps is no longer dependent upon shore bases or airfields, as it has the use of advanced vertical/short take-off and landing (VSTOL)

Harrier AV-8B fighter and ground-attack aircraft and carrier-borne F-18 Hornet fighter aircraft.

The Expeditionary Units were also made special operations-capable (MEU-SOC), with much of their training preparing them for low-intensity conflicts. A study undertaken in the early 1980s noted that of the 113 cities considered to be important to US interests, 80 were within 100km of the sea. The MEU-SOCs are trained to undertake no less than 18 distinct types of missions including amphibious raids, show-of-force operations, the deployment of mobile training teams, civic action and disaster relief tasks, and emergency hostage-rescue operations. In a major operation the lightly equipped Rangers and airborne forces may go in first, but it is the Marines' self-sustaining capabilities that are all important for prolonged hostilities. This was the major reason that General Westmoreland preferred the Marines to airborne forces in Vietnam.

At a stroke the Marines had enveloped 80 per cent of the island

The Marines' ability to use their powerful integrated forces for rescue operations was put to the test in October 1983. A coup on the small Caribbean island of Grenada had trapped 1000 American citizens, mostly medical students. The previous government of Prime Minister Maurice Bishop had developed strong links with the Eastern Bloc and Cuban military advisors were known to be on the island. The new 16-man Revolutionary Military Council represented a significant lurch to the left, and America's worst fears were confirmed on 19 October when the new regime executed Bishop and several cabinet ministers. America was asked to intervene by the Organisation of Eastern Caribbean States and duly accepted, the job of mounting the operation being given to the Commander-in-Chief Atlantic (CINC-LANT). A Marine Amphibious Unit (MAU) and a carrier group, led by the formidable USS *Independence*, were fortunately en route to the Mediterranean when the CINCLANT planning group diverted them to a grid reference off the coast of Grenada. The final plan called

for the Rangers and 82nd Airborne to take Point Salines air base in the early hours of 25 October and move quickly through the southern half of the island. The Marines, with 20 per cent of the 6500-strong invasion force, would secure the northern end.

The final script might have been written by the Marines or the many supporters of the Corps. At Salines itself the airborne pathfinder teams ran into difficulties, and successive waves of Rangers encountered stiffer resistance than expected. A Sea-Air-Land (SEAL) reconnaissance team reported that the beach next to Pearls Airport was just passable to shallow-hulled landing craft but not ordinary ships. The Marines took their first objectives by helicopter. 'Fox' Company landed unopposed at Grenville, while 'Echo' Company encountered light resistance at the airfield. Intelligence was poor and the landing zones (LZs) were boggy, but the targets were taken within 30 minutes. The paratroopers were still held up at Salines and several SEAL/Delta Force special operations had come to grief, but the irrepressible Marines kept moving forward.

At last light, 'Golf' Company was landed at Grand Mal Bay on the other side of the island and close to the capital, St George's. 'Golf' was quickly reinforced by 'Fox' Company, airlifted by helicopters from Pearls Airport — at a stroke the Marines had enveloped 80 per cent of the island. In the early hours of the 26th, the Marine advance rescued the Governor-General and the SEAL team that had tried to evacuate him. The following morning the Marines linked up with the airborne forces as the last pockets of resistance around Grand Anse Campus were eliminated by fighter aircraft from the USS *Independence*.

An MEU arrived in the Gulf soon after the Iraqi Army overran Kuwait

The US Marines and airborne troops joined forces again to provide the political trip-wire that deterred an Iraqi invasion of Saudi Arabia in 1990. An MEU arrived in the Gulf soon after the Iraqi Army overran the small oil state of Kuwait on 2 August. As the momentum of Operation 'Desert Shield' grew, the MEU was

Above: Marines in Saudi Arabia practise firing an M224 60mm mortar. Marine units spearheaded the assault to liberate Kuwait in the Gulf War.

joined by the 1st (Hawaii) and 7th (California) MEBs, and finally the parent 1st and 2nd Marine MEFs — a total of 500 M-60 tanks, 300 aircraft and helicopters and 90,000 Marines, of whom 16,000 (4th MEB) stood ready off the coast of Kuwait in landing ships. The threat was sufficient to unbalance the Iraqis, who prepared for amphibious landings around Kuwait City. Numerous assault landings and special operations on Faylakah Island off the Kuwaiti coastline completed the deception.

The prelude to the liberation of Kuwait (Operation 'Desert Storm') included another deception involving the build-up of Allied forces on the border where the three countries meet, but it was the 1st and 2nd Marine Divisions which punched a hole through the grim obstacle belt in front of the Iraqi lines. The Marines were on the right flank and under the protection of the 16-inch guns of the massive 'Iowa' class battleship *Missouri*. Funnelling in behind them came Saudi, Kuwaiti and Qatari forces on their dash along the coast road to Kuwait City. As the Marines and the 'heavy' American VII Corps plunged deep into the desert, tens of thousands of Iraqis chose to surrender rather than engage this massive force and supporting air power. Kuwait was free again.

The US Marine Corps is currently being restructured to prepare for operations in the twenty-first century. Currently, it has an authorised strength of 195,300 personnel (including 10,500 women), of whom 134,000 are deployed in the operational arm of the Corps — the Fleet Marine Force. The three Marine Aircraft Wings have a combined total of 486 fixed-wing aircraft and 468 helicopters. Amphibious landings are supported by a range of specialised ships whose main task is to quickly land battalions of assault infantry. Most have broad, flat upper decks to accommodate VSTOL aircraft or helicopters and all but the landing platforms helicopter (LPH) carry landing craft. The

LPHs are used for vertical assaults employing helicopters. The others carry troops, vehicles, tanks and stores, either transferring them to landing craft — landing ships dock and landing platforms dock (LPDs/LSDs) — or landing by direct beaching — landing ships, tanks (LSTs). Most landings employ both helicopter-borne forces for vertical envelopment of the beach-head and seaborne forces in landing craft, air-cushioned landing craft (LCAC) or the 1300 lightly armoured AAV-7A1 amphibious tractor (Amtrac) currently in the Corps' arsenal.

Each Marine battalion consists of a head-quarters company, three rifle companies (each divided into 13-man squads) and a weapons company. The standard infantry weapons are the M16A2 rifle with a 40mm grenade launcher attached, and the lightweight 5.56mm squad automatic weapon (SAW) issued to each fire-team. Immediate support is provided by the eight Weapons Company fire-team vehicles armed with 0.5 inch and MK19 40mm heavy machine guns. Heavy support includes M-60 tanks, 155mm towed and self-propelled (SP) howitzers, 8in SP howitzers, 81mm and 60mm mortars and tube-launched, optically-tracked, wire-guided (TOW) anti-tank missile launch-ers. Air-defence weapons included the effective

man-portable Stinger and Redeye surface-to-air missile (SAM) systems.

While the MEU-SOCs are currently trained for special operations, the Corps maintains a dedicated unconventional warfare outfit known as the 'Recons'. Recon units are divided into Force Recon Company and Battalion Recon Company groups. Force Recon deploys four-man teams for a diverse range of special operations: long-range reconnaissance patrols (LRRPs), target acquisition for artillery and naval gunfire, beach reconnaissance, forward aircraft controlling (FAC) and raids. All members are very highly skilled combat swimmers,

parachutists and small boat handlers. Each man is also trained in two or more team specialities (demolitions/signals/medic/special weapons and equipment). Force Recon is tasked by the landing force commander for high-risk strategic missions. Battalion Recon is larger, deploying 500 men in the less specialised role of gathering intelligence on the general area to be used for landings by the parent Marine division.

The SEALs conducted missions under the 'Bright Light' programme

Even more highly trained and specialised are the US Navy SEAL Teams. SEAL Teams One and Two were commissioned by President John F. Kennedy on 1 January 1962 to provide the Navy with an offensive, covert operations unit able to conduct guerrilla and counter-guerrilla warfare, intelligence gathering, combat-rescue and even civic aid or foreign internal defence programmes. These new formations became part of the Naval Special Warfare Groups. They were joined by the existing Underwater Demolition Teams (UDTs) which had seen action in World War II and Korea. While the UDTs had accomplished some offensive operations and intelligence gathering tasks, their special talents were beach reconnaissance and mine clearance.

As the Vietnam War escalated, the UDTs, SEALs and their Special Boat Service colleagues were quickly despatched to support the 'brown water' fleet operating in the canals, estuaries and rivers of South Vietnam. SEAL platoons harried the VC supply lines and camps along the many rivers, operating out of small, armoured river craft. In the Rung Sat area, SEAL platoons disrupted VC and NVA sapper activity so successfully that four more platoons were deployed to carry out surveillance and ambush operations in areas distant from the river. Using the river systems for insertion and exfiltration, the SEALs conducted a number of combat-rescue missions under the 'Bright Light' programme. In late 1970, a team of 15

Left: A barracks ship, with numerous assault and patrol boats alongside, in the Mekong Delta. SEAL units often operated from these vessels.

SEALs and 19 Vietnamese militia stormed a camp in Laos, rescuing 19 South Vietnamese prisoners of war (POWs). It was a Vietnamese SEAL and an American SEAL who rescued Lieutenant-Colonel Hambleton when his electronic warfare plane, 'Bat 21', was shot down in the Song Mieu Giang River area. In all, the SEALs were credited with rescuing 15 POWs and killing some 800 enemy troops. With two Presidential Unit Citations, one Navy and one Meritorious Unit Commendation and 852 personal awards from the Medal of Honor to the Navy Achievement Medal, the SEALs were one of the most decorated units in Vietnam.

SEALs also took part in the 1983 invasion of Grenada, codenamed Operation 'Urgent

Fury', fulfilling important functions on the first day of the invasion — 25 October. Men of SEAL Team Four were tasked with rescuing the Governor-General and taking him to a safe-house, while another SEAL unit were ordered to destroy the transmitter of Radio Free Grenada. At 2200 hours on 25 October, SEALs landed on the northeast coast of Grenada but poor intelligence meant that the missions fared less well than expected. The team sent to shut down the radio walked straight into an ambush, losing two men killed. They were forced to evacuate, having failed to get within range of the radio station. The SEALs sent to rescue the Governor-General also met with disaster; as soon as they arrived at Government House they were surrounded and besieged by Grenadan People's Revolutionary Army (PRA) forces.

The SEALs requested help and, despite the fact that anti-aircraft units were in the area, two AH-1T Cobra helicopters were despatched from the carrier *Guam*. They duly flew into a wall of flak and were both shot down. Undeterred, Admiral Metcalf, commander of the American task force, ordered carrier-borne A-7 aircraft to relieve the SEALs. The aircraft pummelled the anti-aircraft batteries, but they did not kill all the soldiers around Government House. When night came on the 25th, the SEALs were still pinned down.

A company of US Marines stormed ashore at Grand Mal Bay

Metcalf decided to use Marines aboard the landing ship, tank (LST) *Manitowac* to secure the SEALs. In the early hours on the 26th, a company of US Marines stormed ashore at Grand Mal Bay, on the west coast of the island. Mounted on LVTP-7 APCs and supported by five M-60 tanks, they brushed aside light resistance and headed inland. Government House was secured at 0700 hours and the Governor-General was finally evacuated to the *Guam*.

During the 1991 Gulf War, SEAL teams conducted an assortment of missions including beach reconnaissance for possible US Marines landing sites in the event of the land assault into Iraq and Kuwait becoming bogged down. They also conducted deception operations on

Above: SEALs come ashore on a hostile beach.
Far left: SEALs attacking a VC position in Vietnam.

Faylakah Island off the Kuwaiti coast, designed to convince the Iraqis that a large-scale amphibious assault was imminent — this prompted the Iraqis to deploy forces along the coast to deter such an attack. On land, SEAL teams were also involved in the hunt for Iraqi Scud surface-to-surface missiles (SSMs), which were being launched against Israel and Saudi Arabia. Long-range reconnaissance missions by SEAL units were responsible for locating the missiles and then fixing their position using laser designators, which enabled 'smart' ordnance carried by Allied aircraft to pinpoint and then destroy them. Other tasks involved cooperating with British Special Air Service teams and abducting high-ranking Iraqi officers, and also stealing enemy aircraft and surface-to-air missile (SAM) systems for threat-assessment purposes. Overall, the efforts of the SEALs were a major contribution to the eventual Allied victory.

THE BRITISH PARAS

The red beret worn by the British Parachute Regiment is a world-renowned symbol of an elite military unit. From the epic battle at Arnhem to the actions at Goose Green and Wireless Ridge, the paras have proved they are second to none.

JUST after lunch on Sunday 17 September 1944, the sound of an apparently vast armada of aircraft brought the people of the Dutch town of Arnhem into the streets. Since the June landings in Normandy, the Dutch had been anxiously waiting for liberation — in this grim fifth autumn of the war Holland faced starvation. To the west of the town it appeared to be snowing as thousands of British paratroopers left their aircraft in the largest airborne operation ever to be mounted. The people of Arnhem had not expected to see the Allies so quickly. The front was still 130km away and, now that the German Army had been pushed back to the very borders of their homeland, its resolve was stiffening. The very defences that the German elite units had helped breach in 1940 were now being put to good effect as the German Army prepared to defend Holland from behind its maze of canals and rivers.

The capture of the road bridge at Arnhem was intended to complete an 'airborne carpet' that would allow XXX

A 2 Para machine gunner supporting a platoon attack during a training exercise conducted under cover of smoke. The weapon is a belt-fed 7.62mm L7A2 GPMG.

Corps, part of General Miles Dempsey's British Second Army, to breach the German defences on the River Waal and allow the Allies to swing right into the mighty German industrial heartland of the Ruhr, thus hopefully ending the war at the close of 1944. Farther to the south, the 'Screaming Eagles' of the American 101st Airborne had landed to capture the canal bridges between Eindhoven and Veghel. Farther north, their countrymen in the 'All American' 82nd Airborne parachuted in to take the huge bridges over the Rivers Maas and Waal and the Maas-Waal Canal.

Arnhem would be different. To avoid low-lying fenland, the dropping zones (DZs) were far to the west of the town. The United States Air Force (USAF) had insisted on dropping the 1st Airborne Division in daylight and, across Holland, the paratroopers were only dropped on one side of their objectives. Intelligence reports suggested that the 10,000 German troops refitting in the immediate area had been badly mauled in France and Russia, and would therefore offer little resistance. Although this information was correct, the military planners ignored the fact that most of the troops were

Below: An early shot of British paras training at Manchester's Ringway Airport in 1940.

veteran elite motorised or armoured SS units. They had also decided that the paras would fight without the support of 'flying artillery' — tank-busting Typhoon and Tempest fighter-bombers. Battlefield commanders of old valued elite units for their ability to hold 'lost positions' for a few vital hours. Over the next 10 days, the British Parachute Regiment would give that term a completely new meaning.

The first paratroopers to land were the pathfinders of the 21st Independent Company, who cleared and held the dropping and landing zones — resistance was slight. Twenty minutes later, 319 Horsa and Hamilcar gliders arrived carrying the Air Landing Brigade. An hour later, the 'snow' began to fall as the men of the 1st Parachute Brigade leapt into the slipstream. The plan was simple: the paratroops would take the Arnhem bridges and form a defensive box around the town as a bridgehead for the lead elements of XXX Corps.

In the initial landings 39 gliders went missing, the majority carrying the men and jeeps of 1 Airborne Reconnaissance Squadron — the unit supposed to dash to the bridge. Nevertheless, the war still seemed far away when the remaining jeeps, sporting twin Vickers machine guns, set off down the Arnhem road. Their biggest problem appeared to be the thousands

of civilians lining the streets. Behind them came 2 Para with orders to move north of the river on foot and capture the railway and pontoon bridges, before linking up with the reconnaissance squadron. To the north, 3 Para also headed for the road bridge but along the Heelsum-Arnhem road, while most of 1 Para, in reserve, began a long battle march to capture the high ground overlooking the town.

The Germans reacted quickly, though not all in an appropriate manner. Field Marshal Model was enjoying a white wine before lunch at his headquarters on the outskirts of Arnhem when the first Allied aircraft appeared overhead. Within minutes he was fleeing in his staff car believing, wrongly, that the paratroops were part of a force sent to kidnap him. On the other hand, by 1500 hours the 9th SS Panzer Division was quickly moving towards the Allied landing grounds and setting up a defensive ring to the west of the town. The 12 officers and 294 men of SS Panzer Grenadier Reserve Battalion 16 were already positioned between the landing grounds and the bridge. By late afternoon, most of the British paratroops had run into these for-

Below: Operation 'Market Garden'. A British six-pounder anti-tank gun, nicknamed 'Gallipoli', in action against German armour near Oosterbeek.

ces and were engaged in bitter street fighting. By last light, and having seen the two smaller bridges blown up in their faces, only 2 Para had made it to the northern end of the bridge — the British were now effectively cut in two.

At the bridge, repeated attacks reduced Frost's positions to rubble

The bridge itself became the scene of great courage as Lieutenant-Colonel Frost's men, having taken the northern end, twice tried to take the southern end but were driven back by heavy machine-gun fire. The battle started a fire in a German ammunition dump which spread to four trucks and finally the bridge itself. With the night eerily illuminated by the burning bridge and filled with the screams of the dying, further attacks were impossible and so the paras withdrew to set up positions in buildings overlooking the northern end.

Nine days of unmatched courage followed as the paras desperately resisted the German attacks and awaited the arrival of XXX Corps. On Monday, the second lift arrived carrying Brigadier Hackett's 4th Parachute Brigade, but the divisional perimeter was slowly contracting under constant German attack and the British were driven off the LZs. When the RAF

appeared overhead to drop supplies, most fell into the arms of the Germans. At the bridge, repeated German attacks reduced Frost's positions to rubble. When the ammunition ran low, German counterattacks were driven off with bayonets and sheer courage. Most of the paras in these impromptu assaults had already been wounded in the intial battles. Only the dying and severely wounded were moved to makeshift hospitals in the cellars.

The five Victoria Crosses (VCs) won at Arnhem were the mere tip of an iceberg of bravery and endurance, but they provide an lasting record to the nature of the fighting inside the 'cauldron'. Captain Queripel of 10 Para, for example, distinguished himself on the Utrecht road when his unit was dug in. Already wounded in the face when he evacuated a badly wounded noncommissioned officer (NCO) under heavy tank and artillery fire, he returned to lead an assault on a German position which eliminated two machine guns and a captured British anti-tank gun. Fighting from a ditch, Queripel's men repelled wave after wave of Panzer Grenadiers. Finally, with most of his party dead or wounded, the captain, now badly wounded in both arms, remained behind to

cover the withdrawal. He was last seen throwing stick grenades back at the Germans; his actions won him a posthumous VC.

At Arnhem Bridge itself, the efforts of Lieutenant J. H. Grayburn of 2 Para were to result in the award of another VC. He was sent to capture the southern end of the bridge. As he led his platoon across he was met by a hail of gunfire. Hit almost at once, Grayburn nevertheless pressed on until ordered to fall back. The next 48 hours saw courage of the highest kind as he again attempted to lead his men over the bridge. Eventually mortally wounded, his courage in the face of overwhelming fire was not forgotten.

In the final charge, the sappers swept forward firing their Brens from the hip

On the perimeter defences at Oosterbeek, Sergeant Baskeyfield, an anti-tank gunner with the South Staffords (Air Landing Brigade), moved from gun to gun as he fought off repeated assaults by German tanks and infantry. He was killed as the Germans finally broke through. Major Cain of the Northumberland Fusiliers received the only non-posthumous VC of the

operation. Isolated, and fighting with captured weapons, his small party of Fusiliers repeatedly blocked German attacks.

In a battle which had so few survivors, much everyday heroism went almost unnoticed. Brigadier Hackett braved enemy small-arms fire to rescue a wounded staff officer burning to death in a jeep. Lieutenant McKay had already lost 40 of his parachute engineers when he and his remaining 10 men took on 50 Germans and two tanks. In the final charge, the sappers swept forward firing their Brens from the hip. When the smoke finally cleared, only four engineers remained standing.

The RAF lost 84 aircraft in the 601 sorties flown to support the paras. One act of heroism by an aircrew received sufficient notice to win a VC. By the time Flight Lieutenant Lord's Dakota transport aircraft was over the re-supply DZs it was already on fire. British paras below watched the despatchers desperately throwing out the last panniers as the flames engulfed them. The aircraft then briefly attempted to climb before crashing in flames. The desperately-needed supplies had fallen amongst the Germans. There were also acts of chivalry as well. Much of the captured rations and supplies were distributed to the Dutch, and the fighting was frequently stopped to allow the evacuation of British wounded. At the bridge, SS Panzer Grenadiers evacuated the last British wounded, plying them with brandy and chocolate and congratulating them on holding out against such overwhelming odds.

The British Guards Armoured Division finally arrived but were unable to cross the river. On Monday 25 September, the survivors, without food and with only rain water to drink, began to withdraw under the cover of XXX Corps' guns. The parachute brigades had been reduced to the size of companies, while the Air-Landing Brigade could only muster a battalion. Those too badly wounded to walk were left behind to cover the withdrawal. Several thousand men managed to cross the Lower Rhine; others were killed when the Germans discovered what was happening. Some of those unable to cross the river escaped into the countryside, in the hope of being rescued by the MI9 escape organisation. Others fought with the Dutch Resistance, and at least one was captured and sent to a German concentration camp.

Across the street a para OP opened fire killing two terrorists

The Parachute Regiment was to see action again when it parachuted into Germany — codenamed Operation 'Varsity' — in support of the Rhine crossing in February 1945. In the post-war years, a smaller reorganised regiment continued to provide sterling service in the new peacekeeping role. At Suez in 1956, the Regiment was used in the parachute assault role for the last time. Eight years later, the paras were given another 'lost position' to defend, this time in the sandy wastes of South Arabia.

In the early 1960s, a myriad of small independent sheikhdoms that made up the tip of the Arabian Peninsula were amalgamated with the British Colony of Aden into the Federation of South Arabia. In the spirit of post-colonisation Britain had promised the Federation independence, but with the understanding that British troops and bases would remain as a stabilising influence against the rising tide of guerrilla warfare and terrorism. In April 1964, 3 Para had joined the Royal Marine Commandos and other units in a successful operation to isolate rebel tribesmen in the inhospitable mountains of the Radfan region. Two years later, the British Government shocked the Federation's rulers with the sudden announcement that it intended to make a complete withdrawal from the area. 1 Para was now faced with the unenviable chore of helping cover the withdrawal of British forces — a task calling for a totally different type of soldiering.

Their first job was to help kill or capture the FLOSY (Front for the Liberation of South Yemen) terrorists that had begun their own bid for power by killing British servicemen in the markets and narrow alleys in the port of Aden. Parachute Regiment officers were disguised as private soldiers in other regiments and infiltrated into the squalid Sheik Othman quarter with routine infantry patrols. Once inside, paras from C and D Companies established a number of observation posts (OPs) that overlooked the markets, mosques and major roads.

This approach quickly paid dividends. On 1 June 1966, the terrorists used a general strike as a cover for open insurrection. The first attack came in the early morning when four terrorists threw a Russian grenade at a British patrol on duty outside of the main mosque. As the grenade exploded, the terrorists turned to escape into the crowds of worshippers in the mosque — none of them made it. Across the street a para OP opened fire killing two on the steps; a third was shot dead as he attempted to run into a shop. The fourth terrorist dodged the accurate hail of bullets only to run into the arms of a British patrol. This small incident began a major battle as numerous snipers opened up on all the OPs. During the day-long battle the paras, supported by a few scout cars, out-matched the terrorists in both shooting skills and tactics, inflicting heavy casualties and effectively blocking FLOSY's attempts to seize the town.

On 20 June, the paras were faced with their greatest test when the South Arabian Police mutinied and started killing British soldiers and civilians. The mutiny was based on a false rumour that British soldiers had been used to crush a rebellion by the South Arabian Army. Consequently, it was decided that order should be restored without returning police fire and giving credibility to this lie. The almost suicidal task was given to C Company, who drove into the barracks in open trucks. The paras soon came under sporadic rifle and machine-gun fire which killed one paratrooper and wounded another eight. Still the weapons remained on safe. Inside the camp another four parachutists were wounded as the police were disarmed and stood down. Throughout the entire operation, as comrades and even close friends fell, not a single British soldier returned fire.

The commandos and paras were outnumbered by two to one

In 1982, the Parachute Regiment returned to the battlefield after nearly a decade of peace-keeping tours in Northern Ireland. The Falkland Islands had been seized on 2 April by the Argentine dictatorship, who had quickly installed a garrison of 11,000 men. The assumption that Britain would not embark on a war to recapture the islands proved to be a serious miscalculation. The islands would be retaken, primarily by a combination of three Royal Marine Commandos and two Parachute Regiment battalions — the 'Red and Green Fighting Machine'. When the commandos and paras splashed ashore at San Carlos on D-Day, 21 May, they were outnumbered by two to one. Fighting in terrain that resembled a grimmer version of Dartmoor or the Breacon Beacons, and in a cold, wet, hostile climate, it was clear that some exceptional soldiering would be needed to avoid becoming bogged down in a grim war of attrition.

The object of Operation 'Corporate' was the elimination or surrender of the Argentine garrison on the main island of East Falkland. The majority of the enemy were entrenched on two lines of mountain ridges that defended the bleak westerly approaches to the Islands' capital, Stanley. Brigadier Thompson's initial battle plan was to secure the safe anchorage at San

Above: Members of 2 Para, wearing the famous red berets, deploy around a Browning 0.5in heavy machine gun whilst on exercise in Oman.

Below: The price of victory in the Falklands. The campaign cost the Regiment, including attached personnel, a total of 40 dead and 82 wounded.

Carlos, before allowing 3 Para Brigade and 45 Commando to move forward to Teal Inlet, and establishing 42 Commando and an SAS four-man patrol on Mount Kent. Port Stanley was more than 80km to the east, but the nearest Argentine garrison was 32km to the south at Darwin and Goose Green. These were reported to be held by a company and thought to merit no more than a raid. When London pressed for its capture to secure a high profile victory, Lieutenant-Colonel Herbert ('H') Jones' 2 Para was given orders to march south.

By mid-morning the battalion attack had become bogged down

Darwin and Goose Green lie at the southern end of a narrow, easily defended isthmus at a point where the sea almost divides East Falkland in two. The settlements were held by more than 1200 men of the Argentine 2nd and 12th Regiments, and the 601st Anti-Aircraft Battalion equipped with four 105mm howitzers, two 35mm and six 20mm anti-aircraft guns capable of being used in a ground role, in addition to six 120mm mortars. The settlements also had air support from Pucara and Skyhawk ground-attack aircraft. To make matters much worse, London leaked details of the attack, which was allegedly carried by the BBC World Service as 2 Para 'tabbed' toward the start-line. The Argentine garrison went on full alert.

At 0230 hours on 28 May, A Company, 2 Para, crossed the start-line and started to attack the defences around Burntside House, believed to be occupied by an Argentinian platoon but in fact deserted. At 0310 hours, B Company started their advance on the battalion right, while D Company, in reserve, moved between A and B Companies, also encountering light resistance. As dawn approached, enemy artillery and mortar fire increased and A Company ran into a hail of medium and heavy machine-gun fire from Darwin Hill. The enemy trenches were in open ground, forcing the paras to crawl forward to check the next line of defences. Tactics were

flexible; the training manuals were thrown away and airborne initiative came into play. Occasionally, a Milan round would be used to soften up resistance before the section or platoon charged forward to take the position. At other times the paras crawled forward to within 50m of the Argentine positions, with sections alternatively going to ground to lay down covering fire. But ultimately, the trenches were stormed with sheer aggression and the 'raw' fighting techniques of close quarter combat.

By mid-morning the battalion attack had become bogged down as a result of small-arms and artillery fire. B Company, caught on the exposed slopes overlooking Boca House, was pinned down. A Company had fared no better, facing heavy concentrated fire from enemy trench lines. The commanding officer, 'H' Jones, moved forward to take personal command of A Company's attack and break the deadlock. While conducting a flanking movement with part of his tactical headquarters, Jones was hit by gunfire. Still charging forward firing his Sterling submachine gun, he fell mortally wounded.

Right: A weary 3 Para machine gunner on Mount Longdon. The position had been taken on the night of 11/12 June after a ferocious attack.

Tigers in adversity, the paras used Support Company's Milans to smash the defences at Boca House, while B Company managed to use dead ground to attack the trench lines from the flank. Throughout the assault Pucaras and Skyhawks had bombed and strafed the battalion. Now the wrath of the paras was turned against the aircraft. An attack by Skyhawks was followed by two Pucaras dropping napalm on D Company, but the aircraft were driven off.

Below: A 'stick' of paras inside the fuselage of a C-130 Hercules aircraft await the order to jump.

By nightfall, Darwin was captured and Goose Green surrounded. The splendid victory at Goose Green had opened up a southern route to Stanley. This would be used to distract the Argentine garrison from the direction of the main attack and complete the encirclement of the capital. Major-General Moore, Commander Land Forces Falkland Islands, gave the task of capturing Bluff Cove and Fitzroy to Brigadier Wilson's 5th Infantry Brigade, placing 2 Para under Wilson's overall command. As Wilson prepared to move his brigade on a long overland march to the Cove, the paras again

be supported by the Scimitar and Scorpion light tanks of the Blues and Royals, the 4.5in gun of the frigate HMS *Ambuscade*, two batteries of 105mm artillery and the combined weight of 2 and 3 Para's 81mm mortars. The noisy attack would not only help unlock the gates to Stanley itself, but would also provide a welcome distraction for the Scots Guards' nearby assault on Tumbledown Mountain.

Withering suppressive fire cut into the trench lines

At 2145 hours, D Company crossed the start-line and moved through the Argentine positions on 'Rough Diamond', which had been heavily shelled. There were a few dead but the main enemy force had withdrawn. The paras quickly pressed on as the enemy artillery had targeted their old positions for air-bursts. It had started to snow and, away to south, they could hear the sounds of the battle on Tumbledown. On their right, B and A Companies moved forward to occupy 'Apple Pie'. Shocked and broken by the British artillery fire, the defenders had fled back to the main positions on Wireless Ridge. As D Company now prepared to sweep across the line of Argentine trenches and bunkers on the Ridge, heavy machine guns, Milans and light tanks moved onto 'Apple Pie' to lay down suppressive fire.

As D Company started to roll up some of the last Argentine positions before Stanley, they found themselves in a bloody fight with two companies and a regimental headquarters. To their front, withering suppressive fire cut into the trench lines, so close that one of the leading paras in 11 Platoon was killed by friendly fire. Fighting bunker to bunker, the paras cleared the ridge and dug in to await enemy artillery strikes. At dawn the Argentinians launched the only counterattack of the war. This last serious attempt to hold onto the Falkland Islands was beaten off, despite the fact that 2 Para was seriously short of ammunition. The enemy retreat became a rout. In the early afternoon, 2 Para

used their initiative. Breaking into the deserted Swan Inlet House, the paras used the civilian telephone to contact Bluff Cove to receive the startling news that there were no enemy soldiers garrisoned at the settlement. On that evening, 80 men from 2 Para were crammed into a Chinook helicopter and flown to Bluff Cove. When the battalion move was completed the next day, 2 Para had made the fastest advance of the war, the speed of which even unsettled the planners in General Moore's headquarters.

Bluff Cove and Fitzroy were taken on 2 June. Eleven days later, 2 Para took part in the final battles of the war. On the night of 13/14 June, the battalion was tasked to capture Wireless Ridge, a series of prominent knolls to the southeast of Mount Longdon, already in the hands of 3 Para. The Battalion's new Commanding Officer, Lieutenant-Colonel David Chaundler, had promised the men and officers of 2 Para that they would not have to fight unsupported as they had at Goose Green and Darwin. At Wireless Ridge, the battalion would marched towards Stanley, their steel helmets replaced by the famous red beret.

Currently, 5 Airborne Brigade consists of two of the three Parachute Regiment battalions, the elite Pathfinder Platoon, one Gurkha battalion, one infantry battalion, one armoured reconnaissance regiment, one artillery regiment plus various parachute and air-mobile supporting arms, such as engineers, Army Air Corps personnel and soldiers from the Royal Signals. The distinctive red beret with the silver-winged parachute is the distinguishing mark of the Parachute Regiment, while support troops wear their own unique regimental badge on the same beret. As airborne and special forces must carry most of their equipment into battle, they are issued with large capacity bergens. Capable of carrying loads of 20-50kg, the bergen can be secured below the parachutist's smaller reserve

Below: 2 Para on patrol in the 'bandit country' of South Armagh, Northern Ireland. The paras have undertaken many tours in Ulster since 1969.

'chute and can even be swum across water obstacles, should it be necessary to do so.

On the ground the British para, in common with other airborne forces, is expected to fight with only light support. The venerable L1A1 Self-Loading Rifle (SLR) has now been replaced by the more compact and lightweight 5.56mm SA-80. The new weapon is easy to strip and clean in the field, and its short bullpup design ensures that it can be fired effortlessly from the hip, shoulder or lying prone. Its companion, the Light Support Weapon (LSW), will relegate the rather aged L7A2 general purpose machine gun (GPMG) to the tripod-mounted sustained-fire role. Other para support weapons include 81mm and 51mm mortars, and a range of anti-tank weapons including Milan, Carl Gustav and the 66mm light anti-tank weapon (LAW). In the Falklands conflict, both the Royal Marines and paras demonstrated the versatility of anti-tank weapons, especially Milan, by using them to great effect against Argentinian bunkers and fortified trenches.

US AIRBORNE FORCES

The American 82nd and 101st Airborne Divisions are some of the most highly trained and best equipped light forces in the world and, as the 1991 Gulf War proved, they are masters of modern battlefield mobility.

GENERAL 'Billy' Mitchell advocated using US Army parachute formations as early as 1918, but as the prevailing military doctrine centred on old-fashioned, infantry-orientated warfare, parachutists were seen merely as saboteurs of dubious value and the idea was quickly dropped. However, German and Soviet developments were watched closely by Britain and America, and the then US Chief of Infantry suggested the creation of an American parachute formation in 1939, though it was still unclear how such troops should be used. The Army Air Corps felt that the parachutists should be used under their command as 'airborne Marines', arguing that German paratroops came under the control of the Luftwaffe. The US Army's arguments were more persuasive, however, and so the War Department ordered the inventive Major William Lee to form a parachute test platoon to develop training and selection methods for the new formations.

The Safe Parachute Company's main exhibit at the 1939 World Fair, together with 48 volunteers from the 29th Infantry Regiment, gave a late birth to America's illustrious

Paras of the 82nd Airborne Division landing during a training exercise. During Operation 'Desert Shield' the division was the first US unit to be deployed to Saudi Arabia, in August 1990.

airborne tradition. The company had installed a tower at the fair that offered the public a controlled, wire-guided descent. Designed to give aircrew some experience of parachuting, the test jump began with the 'parachutist' being drawn up to the top of one of the structure's four arms, with the canopy deployed by a large metal hoop. At the instructor's command, the parachute was released, allowing the man to float gently down to a soft padded area around the tower's base. A replica of the tower was built at Fort Benning, Georgia, which became the parachute school and home of America's airborne forces. Tower jumping is still an integral part of the course at Benning and the students are introduced to three replicas of the original used at the World Fair during 'Tower Week'.

Massed display jumps from a Douglas B-18 bomber on 16 August 1940 so impressed US Army planners that they immediately commissioned the 501st Parachute Infantry Battalion. Initially, aircraft, parachutes and support were in short supply — US paratroopers like the German *fallschirmjaeger* packed their own parachutes. The impetus for further expansion was provided by the spectacular German airborne operations in Crete in May 1941. By the end of that year, the 502nd, 503rd and 504th Parachute Battalions had been activated and trained. Each of the four battalions of 34 officers and 412 men then became the nucleus of a three-battalion regiment under the control of Lee's Airborne Command. A more streamlined organisation was formed in August 1942, under the auspices of the 82nd Infantry Division, which had unfortunately been deactivated at the end of the World War I. This, in turn, was subdivided into the 82nd 'All American' and 101st 'Screaming Eagles' Airborne Divisions. These large airborne formations also encompassed airborne artillery and engineers, as well as glider infantry regiments.

Later in the war other airborne divisions were formed: the 17th (1942) arrived in Europe after D-Day, while the 11th (1943) went to the Pacific. The unlucky 13th (1944) was formed too late to see action. In addition to the established divisions, independent regiments were also created. The 503rd Parachute Infantry Regiment, for example, saw action in the Pacific, while the 550th and 551st were trained in Panama before being sent to Italy. Sometimes, battalions split from their parent regiment to take on a rather short-lived, independent existence. This untidy state of affairs deliberately ensured that American paratroops were available to fight in every theatre of war within the shortest possible time.

Ridgway's division was rewarded with combat parachute jumps into Sicily

American paratroops made their first combat jump in North Africa, supporting the Anglo-American 'Torch' landings in November 1942. The former Vichy French protectorates then became a base for the 82nd Airborne which followed in May 1943. Under the command of Brigadier-General Matthew Ridgway, the division, by then comprising the 504th and 505th Parachute Infantry Regiments, the 325th Glider Infantry and the 331 C-47 Dakotas of 12 Troop Carrier Command, underwent a very gruelling training cycle. A few months later, Ridgway's division was rewarded with combat parachute jumps into Sicily and southern Italy on the eve of the Allied invasions. By the time Italy surrendered in September 1943, the American and British paras were experienced in this new form of warfare. Much more importantly, doctrine and tactics had been developed to offset the fact that landing behind enemy lines on the eve of an invasion was often fraught with disaster. Missions had to be chosen with care to allow the parachutists every opportunity to dis-rupt the enemy's defences, secure vital bridges and strongpoints for the invasion, while at the same time preventing them from becoming hopelessly cut off and destroyed by the enemy response. Such meticulous planning would be vital for their next operation, which involved the massed drops of thousands of parachutists in the most important airborne mission of World War II. By September 1943, the British 1st Airborne Division and the US 82nd were on their way back to England to join the newly arrived US 101st Airborne Division. Ahead lay Operation 'Overlord', the Allied invasion of occupied Europe.

Above: American paratroopers inside the fuselage of a C-47 aircraft just prior to being dropped in Normandy to support the D-Day landings.

Below: A machine gun crew of the 101st Airborne Division awaits the German onslaught on the outskirts of Bastogne in December 1944.

The original plans for the Normandy landings had been expanded to include an isolated beachhead — 'Utah' Beach — the capture of which would allow the 4th US Infantry Division to quickly cut off the Cotentin Peninsula, thereby protecting the Allies' right flank. Running parallel to 'Utah' was the River Merderet and a large area of marsh, crossed only by four narrow, easily defended causeways. When Lieutenant-General Omar Bradley, commander of the US First Army, saw the reconnaissance photographs, he requested paratroops to seize the causeways across the marshlands and bridges over the Mederet. He was assigned the 101st Airborne. Ridgway's 82nd would jump farther inland, close to the town of Ste Mère Église, thus sealing off the western half of the peninsula and isolating the port of Cherbourg.

Many pathfinders were forced to set up their beacons under enemy fire

The success of the D-Day parachute landings hinged on the simple necessity of having the aircraft carrying the various formations arrive at the right place at the right time. In Sicily, the problem had been solved by using pathfinder teams. Over Normandy the difficulties were magnified by the weather, concentrated anti-aircraft fire and the sheer size of the airborne armada. The first Allied soldiers to parachute behind the Normandy beaches, on the evening of 5 June 1944, were the American pathfinder teams. Their job was to clear selected dropping zones (DZs) of obstacles, set up the 'Eureka' radio homing beacons and hold against enemy counterattack. In the dark, an hour behind the pathfinders, were the 822 C-47s carrying over 13,000 American paratroops.

Once over occupied territory, the pilots navigated their way across the black landscape using the faint reflections of major roads, bridges, railway lines and rivers as reference points. Close to the DZ, 'Rebecca' receivers in the lead aircraft picked up the radio signals from the many 'Eureka' beacons. As the lead C-47 aircraft crossed the coast, more than one DZ was already under attack and many pathfinders were forced to set up their beacons under often intense enemy fire.

Above: Paratroops of the 187th Airborne Regimental Combat Team drop from C-119 'Flying Boxcars' near Sunchon, October 1950.

Despite the best efforts of the pathfinders, some aircraft were still forced to drop their soldiers 'blind' or on other marked DZs. Flying through heavy anti-aircraft fire, the pilots were forced to leave their tightly packed formations to dodge the flak. Navigators became confused and lost track of their position, while men who were dropped a mere 500m either side of the right DZ became lost in a patchwork of nearly identical fields and hedgerows. Planes that accidentally overshot the DZ were forced to circle, banking steeply and disrupting the heavily laden sticks that were waiting for their chance to jump. Re-entering the tightly packed stream of aircraft was hazardous in the extreme.

Within hours a significant proportion of the 82nd and 101st Airborne Divisions had been widely scattered across most of the Cot-

entin Peninsula, incurring 1500 casualties as men came down in trees, hedgerows, rivers and farm yards from Carentan to Cherbourg. Sticks accidentally dropped over Ste Mère Église were almost entirely wiped out, fatally illuminated by the fires started by Allied bombing as they descended. Elsewhere, small groups of lost parachutists banded together to fight their own war. At first light, most of the initial objectives had been taken, although the airborne cordon around the peninsula was not as secure as was planned. The operation's most powerful effect was the panic and confusion that swept through the German High Command as reports of hundreds of separate battles filtered back from the front. On 'Utah' Beach the landing craft carrying one half of Bradley's First Army met with only light opposition.

The American paratroops remained in the line for three weeks while the beachhead was consolidated. After refitting in England, the two airborne divisions came together again to form the large US component of Operation 'Market Garden' (September 1944). While the 101st were dropped at Veghel, nearest the Allied front line, and were soon enjoying the direct support of the British XXX Corps, the 82nd, dropped a further 20km north at Grave, encountered stiff opposition to their attempts to capture the vital bridges over the Waal at Nijmegen in Holland. When paratroops and tanks of the British Grenadier Guards failed to take the southern end of the road bridge, the 504th Parachute Infantry crossed the fast-flowing river in canvas boats.

St Vith fell but the 101st Airborne held onto Bastogne

Despite losing most of the first wave to heavy enemy fire, the paras secured a toehold on the opposite bank and used it to seize the northern ends of the rail and road bridges. A concerted attack on both ends of the bridge by paratroops

Above: Operation 'Hawthorne', June 1966. The 101st Airborne in action in Kontum Province.

and Guards armour resulted in very bitter fighting as the Germans fought back with anti-tank weapons concealed amongst the steel girders on the bridge. At nightfall, two tanks managed to cross the bridge and link up with the American paras — the last bridge on the road to Arnhem had finally been taken. The British Second Army's commander, General Miles Dempsey, later saluted the 82nd Airborne, referring to it as the 'greatest division in the world today!'

Several months later, the 101st Airborne was also to win fame in a small town in the Belgium Ardennes. In the early morning of 16 December 1944, three German armies moved out of concealed positions in the Eifel Mountains and into the snow-covered forests of the Ardennes. Operation 'Watch on the Rhine' was a daring plan to capture Antwerp by driving a wedge between the American armies in the south from the British and Canadian forces in Belgium and Holland. General Eisenhower responded quickly, sending the US 7th Armoured Division and the 101st Airborne Division to hold the vital road junctions of St Vith and Bastogne. St Vith fell but the 101st Airborne held onto Bastogne, resisting the fierce assault

of the 15th Panzer Grenadier Division which surrounded the town. As the Allied First and Third Armies counterattacked from the north and south, the major weight of the German attack was increasingly funnelled towards the narrow 'bulge' dominated by Bastogne. Hitler's dream of a second Dunkirk died at the small Belgium town. The 101st Airborne held their positions during eight days of brutal fighting, until finally relieved by General Patton's Third Army on 26 December.

Later, while the 17th Airborne Division parachuted across the Rhine with the British 3rd Parachute Brigade, the 82nd and 101st Divisions fought their way across Germany with the infantry. The 82nd remained in Germany after 1945 to police Berlin, but most other airborne formations were subsequently disbanded and absorbed into the 'All Americans'.

Five years later, the US Army experimented with paratroops in Korea. After Japan's surrender in September 1945, the elite 187th Glider Infantry Regiment retrained as parachutists and went to Korea as the 187th Airborne Regimental Combat Team. Parachute assaults were again used to support Allied offensives, but these were often so brisk that the DZs were quickly by-passed. One notable operation in a war with little 'classic' paratrooper action was the combat jump onto two DZs 30km north of Pyongyang, the North Korean capital, to intercept a freight train reportedly evacuating many American prisoners of war (POWs) and senior communists. On 22 October 1950, 1470 paratroops and 74 tons of equipment were landed astride Sunchon's main supply arteries. Two days of intense fighting followed as the paras annihilated the North Korean People's Army (KPA) 239th Infantry Regiment and various other smaller units. As bad weather had delayed the operation, the train escaped. However, a few American survivors were rescued from a group of POWs, most of whom were murdered by the KPA as it withdrew.

The 101st Airborne was reactivated in 1956 and sent its 1st Brigade to Vietnam in 1965. Two years later, the rest of the division followed, but Vietnam was not a paratrooper's war. The 101st launched one major airborne operation in the same year, when the 503rd Parachute Infantry Regiment made a battalion drop to the north of Tay Ninh City as part of Operation 'Junction City' in February 1967. The operation involved the 503rd Parachute Infantry Regiment, units of the 1st and 5th Infantry Divisions, 11th Armoured Cavalry Regiment, 196th Light Infantry Brigade, elements of the 4th and 9th Infantry Divisions, Army of the Republic of Vietnam (ARVN) units, as well as the 173rd Airborne Brigade. The targets were bases north of Tay Ninh City.

The plan involved a sizeable parachute drop being followed up by a large heliborne assault as an immediate back-up. The use of paratroopers also freed helicopter assets which could be used to transport additional infantry units, as well as artillery and ammunition. The 173rd, by parachuting in, freed 60 UH-1H 'Huey' and eight CH-47 Chinook helicopters. A total of 13 C-130 Hercules transport aircraft were used to drop the men, with another eight dropping their equipment.

One battalion undertook an airmobile assault

The assault went in on the morning of 22 February, with the subsequent helicopter operations maintaining the overall momentum of the attack. The combined operations begun by the 173rd continued until mid-May, by which time the Viet Cong (VC) had lost 2700 dead, large quantities of ammunition, medicines and supplies, as well as over 800 tons of rice.

The 1st Brigade of the 101st Airborne Division arrived in South Vietnam on 29 July 1965 from Fort Campbell, Kentucky. They were quickly employed in securing the An Khe base area for the 1st Cavalry Division. During Operation 'Highland' (22 August-2 October 1965) one 101st battalion undertook an airmobile assault, in conjunction with a battalion-size ground attack, to open the An Khe Pass and to secure Route 19 from Qui Nhon to An Khe. However, by 1966 the 101st was learning heli-

Left: Wounded men of the 1st Brigade, 101st Airborne Division, near An Khe in September 1965.

Above: Artillerymen of the 82nd Airborne Division firing an M102 105mm howitzer at Port Salines during the October 1983 invasion of Grenada.

copter assault techniques and trading in its parachutes for rotary-wing aircraft; it had, in effect, ceased to be a parachute formation.

As each aircraft made its approach it came under heavy fire

Vietnam witnessed a change in direction concerning American airborne operations, with the emphasis moving away from mass parachute drops. Fast tactical deployment by helicopter was in many instances preferable to strategic deployment by parachute, as the former allowed troops to be moved rapidly from one area of operations to another. Once on the ground a parachute unit is virtually immobile, and was therefore totally unsuited to the type of fighting seen in Vietnam, where there were no front lines as such and the enemy was extremely elusive. In Vietnam, along with the 1st Cavalry Division, the 101st Airborne was designated 'Airmobile' and used in the offensive support role. In October 1974, the 'Screaming Eagles' were officially designated the 101st Airborne Division (Air Assault).

The 82nd Airborne also saw action in Vietnam, serving for 22 months between 1968-69, during which time it played an important role in countering the Tet Offensive launched in January 1968. In the early 1970s it was made an integral part of the Americn Rapid Deployment Force. In those days, the parachute-capable 82nd Airborne seemed ideally suited to mount a quick response to possible Soviet aggression in the Middle East or to help reinforce US forces in Germany should a major conflict break out in central Europe.

The 82nd Airborne's main contribution to Operation 'Urgent Fury' in Grenada in 1983 was to reinforce the two Ranger battalions at Point Salines airfield, before moving forward to rescue American students at the True Blue Medical and Grand Anse campuses of the St George's University Medical School, located between the airfield and the island's capital, St George's. That these tasks were all accomplished within 48 hours says much for the 82nd Airborne's training and readiness.

The first elements of the division arrived over Point Salines, on the west of the island, at mid-morning to find the eastern end of the runway still held by Grenadan militia and their

Above: 'Just Cause'. Two soldiers of the 82nd
Airborne in action on the streets of Panama City.

many Cuban advisors. As each aircraft made its
approach it came under heavy fire, and the
small runway could only handle one aircraft at a
time. Meanwhile, the continuous stream of C-
130 Hercules and C-141 Starlifters were forced
to circle the island several times, with some
having to refuel at Puerto Rico. After a savage
five-hour battle, the Rangers and 82nd Airborne secured the airfield and were finally able

to reach the medical school campus by nightfall. Other students, many living at Grand Anse
and at boarding houses in St George's, were
located and evacuated during the following day.

On 20 December 1989, US forces stormed
into tiny Panama to bring its dictator, Manuel

Noriega, back to the United States to face drug trafficking charges. Unwilling to contemplate a protracted war, the United States invaded Panama with five task forces consisting of 11,500 troops, who were charged with seizing or destroying a total of 27 different targets.

The 82nd Airborne formed an integral part of three sub-operations. A few minutes after midnight, the first aircraft carrying the Rangers and paratroops of 'Task Force Red' came in low and fast over Omar-Torrijos airport. Shooting had already begun throughout the country as Delta and SEAL units moved to cut off Nori-

Below: Operation 'Desert Shield'. A soldier of the 82nd Airborne Division mans a TOW anti-tank missile launcher in the desert of Saudi Arabia.

ega's known escape routes. A few minutes after midnight, soldiers of a reinforced Ranger battalion left their aircraft to secure the airport and adjoining military airstrips. They were met by the Panamanian Defence Force's (PDF) 2nd Rifle Company and three armoured vehicles. Behind the Rangers came the 82nd Airborne, flying at 150m, with a C-141B arriving every 10 seconds. On the ground, the three armoured vehicles had been destroyed by the Rangers and a circling Special Operations C-130 gunship. As the battle raged through the new passenger terminal, 20 more C-141B transports arrived carrying two more battalions of the 82nd Airborne ('Task Force Pacific'). These quickly moved through the airport to secure bridges over the Pacora River, isolating Panama City

from the east. An additional consignment of M551 Sheridan tanks were heavy-dropped to lend their weight to the many firefights. Light but impervious to small-arms fire, these old, unpopular tanks routed several intense PDF counterattacks.

The paratroops spent another day in Tocumen City mopping up sporadic pockets of resistance before fighting their way through to 'Task Force Bayonet' in Panama City. Meanwhile, in eastern Panama, other elements of the 82nd and the 7th Light Infantry ('Task Force Atlantic') had taken a number of key installations, including the vital Madden Dam and Sierra Tigre power plant, while providing protection for US bases in Colon. The sporadic fighting by Noriega's 'Dignity Battalions' con-

tinued for several weeks in Panama City, but order was finally restored when the 82nd Airborne helped to winkle out the last pockets of resistance. Noriega himself surrendered to American custody on 3 January 1990 and was flown to Florida to face drugs charges.

The helicopters of the 101st Division raced north to the Tigris-Euphrates

US airborne forces were the first units to be deployed to Saudi Arabia during Operation 'Desert Shield', in response to the invasion of tiny Kuwait by Iraq in August 1990. During the whole of that month, Galaxy and Starlifter aircraft flew the 82nd Airborne Division and all its equipment to Dhahran air base in Saudi Arabia. In September, ships carrying the 101st Airborne Division's equipment and 350 helicopters arrived in the country. Both these divisions were part of XVIII Airborne Corps and, prior to the Allied assault, were secretly moved west along Iraq's undefended border.

On 23 February 1991, the Allied drive to free Kuwait began. XVIII Corps leapfrogged by air and land into Iraq, establishing large fuel and supply dumps deep inside enemy territory. The helicopters of the 101st Division raced north to the Tigris-Euphrates Valley and quickly seized the important town of Al Nasiriya, thus cutting off the retreating Iraqis in Kuwait and southern Iraq. XVIII Corps then swung east, outflanking and destroying the elite Iraqi Republican Guard and other Iraqi units in a series of short battles. Kuwait was liberated by 25 February and the Americans called a ceasefire on the 27th. Operation 'Desert Storm' had been a resounding success, not least because of the efforts of US airborne forces.

Currently, the 82nd Airborne Division is composed of three airborne infantry brigades, divisional artillery and seven additional support battalions — a total of 13,000 men. The 'on call' status rotates through the division and the 82nd remains ready to deploy worldwide at 'no notice'. As a matter of pride, almost all the division's 18,000 troops are parachute-trained and wear the maroon beret, 'Airborne' shoulder tab, as well as the very distinctive 'All American' shoulder flash.

THE ISRAELI PARACHUTE CORPS

Israel's airborne troops have been involved in some of the Jewish state's most savage battles. From the heroism at the Mitla Pass to the capture of East Jerusalem , the Israeli paras have proved themselves to be an elite.

T HE Israeli Parachute Corps can claim to be descended from a handful of brave Jewish fighters who parachuted into occupied Europe in 1945. As part of a deal struck between GHQ Cairo and the Jewish underground (*Haganah*), Romanian and Hungarian Jews were recruited to establish a clandestine escape line in the Balkans. The Royal Air Force (RAF) intended to use the line to rescue Allied aircrew shot down over hostile territory, but the unofficial aim of some of the operatives was the rescue of Jews trapped in Hungary. Many of these intrepid units were captured and either shot or sent to concentration camps. The Hanna Szenes party parachuted into Yugoslavia from where they were conducted across the Hungarian border by partisans. Captured during a routine document check at a railway station, Szenes was taken to Budapest and executed. Another of the party, Yoel Palgi, escaped from the train taking him to a concentration camp

Israeli paras on a beach landing zone following a successful anti-terrorist raid into Lebanon. Their Sikorsky CH-53 Sea Stallion helicopter can be seen in the background.

and made his way back to Palestine. Three years later, he was given the task of forming the Israeli Parachute Corps.

War in Palestine had become increasingly likely. The Jews' long dispute with their Arab neighbours over the creation of a Jewish home-land reached a climax in November 1947 when the Arab countries rejected the United Nations (UN) partition of Palestine. British occupying forces withdrew on 14 May 1948 and President David Ben-Gurion duly proclaimed the State of Israel. As the fighting intensified, Ben-Gurion commissioned the first parachute unit on 26 May as part of his vision of a range of elite units which would defend Israel.

Equipped with only a single Curtiss C-46 Commando aircraft, a small supply of para-chutes and the old RAF base at Ramat David, Major Palgi was expected to produce a com-pany of fully trained paratroops. Among his 100-odd recruits were experienced *Pal'mach* fighters (a guerrilla-type force established in World War II by the British and the Jews to operate behind German lines if the latter's army invaded Palestine), French Foreign Leg-ionnaires, American paras and an assortment of concentration camp survivors, speaking more than a dozen languages and with mixed combat experience. The fledgling paratroops were not

Below: *Pal'mach* troops in action during the 1948 war. Many of these hardy troops joined the paras.

to see combat during the 1948 War of Ind-ependence. Major Palgi and his recruits were despatched to Czechoslovakia where, disguised as Czech soldiers, they underwent infantry and parachute training. When the fighting ended in July, the Israelis were still in Czechoslovakia.

Having missed the opportunity to prove itself in battle, the unit had to fight hard for survival. With the fighting over, the General Staff was reluctant to maintain an elite unit that required many scarce resources. A new com-mander, Colonel Yehudah Harari, tightened discipline and formed Israel's first parachute school at Tel Nof airfield so that Israel could train its own paratroops. When the first class finished their 36-day course with a parachute drop over the beach at Jaffa, David Ben-Gurion accorded the unit recognition by personally presenting the men with their maroon berets and parachute wings.

By the end of the 1940s, as a consequence of the defeat of the Arab armies, two-thirds of Palestine's Arabs were living in squalid refugee camps in Jordan and the Gaza Strip. These Palestinians became the focus of a different type of war, one fought by guerrillas (*fedayeen*) who raided the agricultural settlements along Israel's borders. Israel in turn conducted its own raids against the guerrilla bases, though Colonel Harari's repeated requests to employ his parachute brigade on these nightly raids were denied. GHQ considered the Israeli

Above: Armed with aged Sten guns, these Israelis await an Egyptian attack in the Sinai, 1956.

Defence Force (IDF) to be poorly motivated and generally unreliable, and so chose instead to form a small commando unit under the able leadership of Ariel 'Arik' Sharon, an experienced intelligence officer. He recruited several old comrades for an experimental reprisal raid against the Arab village of Nebi Samwil. The raid was a success and, as a result, Sharon's force was expanded to a 45-man commando unit and given the designation Unit 101.

After narrowly avoiding destruction on one of its first raids against an Egyptian intelligence outpost in the Gaza camp of El-Bureij, Unit

101 went on to launch many raids into enemy territory. Other operations were launched in conjunction with the paratroops, Harari having at last persuaded the General Staff to allow his unit to see combat. However, Harari's very success turned into a personal defeat. The large

Above: In the 1973 war the paras served as mechanised infantry. Here, they advance in the Sinai.

numbers of Arab casualties during the reprisal operations — over 100 were killed or wounded at El-Bureij alone — led to criticism of Unit 101's methods. After just four months of combat, the Unit was deactivated and absorbed into the larger 890th Parachute Battalion. The General Staff, impressed by Sharon's aggressive commando tactics, gave him overall command of the paratroops. Harari resigned in protest.

Under Sharon's command the paratroops were expanded and turned into an elite force. The guerrilla raids continued and so further retaliatory strikes were launched against Gaza, Khan Yunis, Kalkilya, Azun and other camps inside Jordan. In 1956, Israel was given the opportunity to strike a major guerrilla sponsor when Anglo-French forces prepared to invade Egypt in retaliation for its seizure of the Suez Canal. Israel decided to strike first, engaging the Egyptian Army before it could be reinforced and using its elite 202nd Parachute Brigade to paralyse communications between the Sinai Peninsula and Egypt.

Left: Jerusalem, June 1967. A member of the 55th Reserve Parachute Brigade edges forward.

On the evening of 29 October, 16 C-47 Dakotas and Nord Atlas aircraft of the Israeli air force took off from bases in Israel and flew low across the Sinai Desert. Inside the troop carriers were 395 men of the 890th Battalion of the 202nd Parachute Brigade. Their objective was the Mitla Pass, a vital road junction in the sand hills to the east of the Canal and 300km behind enemy lines. In order to achieve total surprise, no prior reconnaissance of the area had been conducted. Once on the ground, and against whatever odds they faced, the battalion was tasked with capturing the eastern end of the Pass and holding it until the balance of the brigade arrived overland.

Flying low to avoid Egyptian radar, the transports and their fighter escort arrived over the Parker Memorial at the eastern end of the Pass at around 1700 hours. Climbing to 200m, the aircraft levelled out and the battalion commander, Raful Eitan, jumped out into the slipstream to begin the first action of the Sinai campaign. Surprise was total. Despite being dropped 5km from the dropping zone (DZ), the eastern end of the Pass was secure by 1930 hours and at 2100 hours the Dakotas returned to drop the unit's jeeps, 106mm anti-tank guns, medium mortars and ammunition.

Within minutes Israeli vehicles and dead blocked the narrow defile

A few hours before midnight, the remainder of the 202nd Brigade moved out in a convoy of half-tracks, jeeps and French AMX-13 light tanks. Between the Israeli lines and Mitla were three heavily defended strongpoints. The first Egyptian outpost was overrun without a fight, and the second desert base at Themed was captured around dawn in a 40-minute battle that cost the lives of four Israelis and 50 Egyptian soldiers. The third strongpoint, Nakhl, fell in the afternoon, allowing Sharon to link up with his airborne spearhead at dusk.

Almost immediately, the tireless Sharon decided to push farther west, despatching a *Nahal* battalion (Fighting Pioneer Youth) to reconnoitre the Pass. Within minutes Israeli vehicles and dead blocked the narrow defile, caught in a merciless hail of fire from the surrounding cliffs. Hidden in the caves and crannies was the 5th Battalion of the Egyptian 2nd Infantry Brigade. The paratroops would later discover no less than 12 artillery pieces, 40 self-propelled guns and 14 heavy machine guns hidden inside the Pass. To add to the devastation, Egyptian air support in the shape of four Meteor jets strafed and bombed the column as it attempted to withdraw. Unable to retreat, the tanks and half-tracks following the *Nahal* paratroops forced their way through the narrow defile to the western opening. Sharon's force was now divided into three, with the tanks and half tracks to the west, the *Nahal* paratroops caught in the ambush in the centre and the rest of the Brigade still at the eastern opening.

The 202nd Brigade was committed to the battle of Rafah Junction

With a recce unit in position on the top of the cliffs, an Israeli volunteer drove an unarmoured jeep back into the Pass and gave his life to allow the recce team to pinpoint the Egyptian positions. That night Sharon's paratroops moved along the cliff face, clearing the enemy strongpoints with grenades and small-arms fire. At dawn, with more than 260 Egyptian soldiers dead, the Pass was finally in Israeli hands. The Israelis had lost 38 killed and 120 wounded in one of the fiercest actions of the war.

In the period between 1956 and 1967, the combat-proven Parachute Corps was enlarged and reorganised into three brigades — one regular and two reserve. All three were highly trained in both parachute and heliborne assault. Against a background of continual border clashes, Syria and Egypt, strengthened by Soviet military aid, adopted an increasingly menacing posture. Finally, in response to an Egyptian blockade of the Straits of Tiran, Israel launched a pre-emptive strike on 5 June 1967 (the Six Day War). When Jordan entered the war in support of the rest of the Arab League, the IDF faced a war on three fronts: Sinai, the Golan Heights and the West Bank.

The 202nd Brigade, now commanded by Raful Eitan, was committed to the battle of Rafah Junction as mechanised infantry, mounted on M3 half-tracks. Elsewhere, the port of

Sharm el-Sheikh, returned to Egyptian control under pressure from the UN, was retaken by a combined air and sea assault. An initial marine and helicopter force encountered little opposition and the paratroops were air-landed after the port was back in Israeli hands.

One reserve parachute brigade was assigned to the army division now commanded by Ariel Sharon. At Abu Aghelia in northern Sinai, Sharon's division faced a formidable defensive position held by the Egyptian 2nd Infantry Division. In an imaginative plan, the paratroops were used to weaken the defences by destroying the covering Egyptian artillery. Pathfinder teams, dropped at night, cleared a large helicopter landing zone (LZ) just four kilometres from the enemy batteries. Within minutes the first aircraft of a continuous helicopter shuttle arrived to off-load their paratroops. As one helicopter disappeared another landed, in what was the first brigade airborne operation in the history of the Corps. As the rest of Sharon's division launched their frontal assault, the paras

Below: Defence Minister Dayan, with eye patch, with Israeli officers at the Suez Canal in October 1973, following their successful counterattack.

attacked. Within an hour the Egyptian artillery had been destroyed, as platoons of parachutists attacked individual artillery pieces.

The other unit, the 55th Reserve Parachute Brigade under the command of Motta Gur, the *Nahal* battalion commander at Mitla Pass, was given the most emotive task of the war. In order to relieve the Israeli half of Jerusalem, which was under heavy bombardment by Jordanian artillery, Motta Gur was ordered to take the Old City itself. At 0215 hours on 6 June, the para brigade started to cut its way through the border fences. The leading 66th Battalion was detailed to eliminate the strongpoints at the Police School and the heavily defended trench lines on Ammunition Hill, which, together, dominated all the approaches into the city from the north and east. At dawn the battle for the Hill was still raging, with frightful casualties being inflicted on both sides. Israeli attacks were met with counterattack and ambush. At the climax of the battle, the paras, advancing behind Sherman tanks, were able to get close enough to the last enemy bunkers to lay demolition charges.

Unaware of the carnage on Ammunition Hill, the rest of Motta Gur's brigade finally

Above: In the Lebanon, June 1982. The para in the foreground holds an RPG-7 anti-tank weapon.

cleared Sheikh Jarrah and Mount Scopus. In ruthless street fighting, Israeli tanks fired at point-blank range into pockets of resistance. Doors were smashed in and buildings cleared to provide positions for suppressive fire to support the assault on the next strongpoint. Finally, the Old City was taken on 7 June by an attack through the Lion's Gate. Israeli soldiers were able to pray at the Wailing Wall for the first time in 19 years.

At the end of the Six Day War, hostilities continued in the shape of terrorism, guerrilla warfare and the shelling of Israeli positions on the eastern side of the Suez Canal, a period of low-intensity operations known as the War of Attrition. The Israeli paras were assigned a role in countering all of these forms of aggression

and, in so doing, achieved international fame as a commando force. In an attempt to persuade the Egyptians to cease hostilities, the paras launched a series of lightning raids against the Nadja'a-Hamadi electrical power station and a number of bridges around the Aswan Dam. Other raids followed, one directed against a fortified anti-aircraft position at the mouth of the Suez Canal, while in another brilliant operation a *Nahal* parachute battalion hijacked an entire Soviet-built P-12 'Spoonrest' radar installation from a fortified site at Ras Gharib in December 1969.

The paras crossed the canal in rubber assault craft

Israel found itself at war again in 1973, when Syria and Egypt launched an offensive during the Jewish religious festival of Yom Kippur on 6 October. In response, the regular parachute brigade was quickly flown to the Gulf of Suez to block Egyptian armoured thrusts towards the Abu Rodeis oil fields. One reserve brigade

found itself holding the Mitla and Jiddi Passes, while the other reserve brigade was committed to the fighting around Mount Hermon on the Syrian border.

As the fighting progressed, the reserve paras holding the Passes were chosen to spearhead a counter-offensive across the Suez Canal at Deversoir on 16 October. The paras crossed the canal in rubber assault craft, despite ferocious artillery fire which destroyed most of the Israeli armour marshalling on the east bank. Exposed on the Egyptian side of the Canal, the paras waited for Major-General Ariel Sharon's division with its tanks and bridging equipment to link up with them. However, by now the Egyptian 16th Infantry and 21st Armoured Divisions had blocked all the approach roads to the Canal. The impasse was broken when the regular 202nd Brigade, despatched from the Gulf of Suez, attacked the Egyptian positions at the 'Chinese Farm' — a former Japanese agricultural station on the Canal approaches.

The 'Farm', an Egyptian divisional headquarters, was taken at a terrible cost as first

artillery and then tank and heavy machine-gun fire were brought to bear on the paras. A survivor later reported that the shells hurtled in with the tempo of machine-gun fire. Finally, a combined force of paratroops and tanks cleared a narrow corridor to the Canal. On the other side of the Canal, the reserve brigade was also under heavy attack by elements of the Egyptian 182nd Brigade. Artillery strikes were followed by air attacks, helicopter assaults and finally raids by Egyptian commandos, who fought the paras in savage battles of mutual annihilation. Nevertheless, the cease-fire approached with the Israelis still holding their little corner of the African continent.

However, just days before the cessation of hostilities, one vital position still remained to be recaptured — Mount Hermon. During the Six Day War Israeli troops had taken the lower southwestern peaks, establishing a fortified radar installation that covered most of Syrian and Jordanian airspace. In the early afternoon of Yom Kippur, the Syrian army used its positions on the summit to launch a heliborne assault by

a ranger battalion and elements of the elite Syrian 82nd Parachute Battalion. The Israeli defenders held out all afternoon but, just as the sun was setting, a group of Syrian commandos finally scaled the walls with ropes and grappling hooks and poured into the underground chambers to end the siege.

The fort remained in Syrian hands despite repeated counterattacks by *Golani* infantry and an Israeli offensive on the plains below that penetrated 30km into Syrian territory. With the cease-fire approaching, the 'Eyes of Israel' looked likely to remain under Arab control. On 21 October, the Israelis launched a last-ditch counterattack, landing a reserve paratroop brigade on the summit, while *Golani* infantry stormed the Syrian positions from below. The Arab commandos fought back valiantly, knocking out most of the *Golani* armour with Soviet rocket-propelled grenades and, despite being caught between the paras and *Golani* units, the Syrians fought throughout the night. Finally, at 1000 hours the next morning and a short time before the cease-fire was due to take effect, a last *Golani* assault, supported by close artillery fire, overwhelmed the defenders.

The Yom Kippur War caught the Israelis by surprise and forced them to rethink their tactics. Another type of elite unit that had maintained a distant connection with the Parachute Corps found themselves caught up in the reorganisation that followed the 1973 conflict. These were the *Sayeret* units formed to conduct long-range reconnaissance/surveillance patrols and various special operations along Israel's fragile borders. *Sayeret Shaked* (Recce 'Almond') was formed in 1961 under the command of a Bedouin scout, Lieutenant-Colonel Majed Chader, who took the Hebrew name Amos Yarkoni. *Shaked* personnel wore paratroop uniforms with a distinctive black beret and Samson's foxes on their shoulder flashes. The unit had its own air support, consisting of light civil aircraft equipped with machine guns, while commando raids and other special operations were carried out by a special elite squad

designated *Shefifon* ('rattlesnake'). The Central and Northern territorial commands (*Sayarot*) maintained their own elite reccce units. *Sayeret Charuv* operated against terrorists in the Judean and Sumerian hills, while *Sayeret Egoz* was deployed in the north.

After the Yom Kippur War, some of the *Sayaret* units were attached to various brigades as mechanised infantry, while others, such as the elite counter-terrorist unit *Sayeret Mat'kal*, kept their independence under the direct command of GHQ. Currently, *Sayeret Orev* is a reconnaissance anti-armour unit attached to the

Right: Equipped with gas mask and Galil, a para combats rioters on the occupied West Bank.

Left: Men from the 35th Parachute Brigade on patrol near Sidon, 1982. The paras had made an amphibious landing near the Awali River on 7 June.

soldiers — rescue seemed impossible. The first Israeli commandos to arrive was a Mossad team deployed to support the main rescue force. In the early hours of 4 July, four C-130 aircraft landed at Entebbe carrying a *Sayeret Mat'kal* hostage-rescue unit and elements of the 35th Parachute and *Golani* Brigades. While the anti-terrorist force rescued the hostages, killing 13 terrorists at the cost of only one man, the infantry blocked Ugandan reinforcements and dismantled various pieces of Soviet hardware, which were then taken back to Israel. The entire operation was completed in 53 minutes.

Another *Sayeret* unit achieved international fame when Israel responded to Lebanese-based terrorist attacks with two offensives: Operation 'Litani' in 1978 and Operation 'Oranim' in 1982. 'Oranim' (Peace For Galilee) was a full-scale invasion of Lebanon to eliminate terrorist bases and sanctuary areas. The offensive, which involved all Israel's armed services, began on 6 June with armoured thrusts deep into Lebanon.

On the ground, one strongpoint, held by the Syrian Army and the PLO Kastel Brigade, had been by-passed. This was Beaufort Castle, a twelfth-century fort that overlooked the Litani River gorge in southern Lebanon. Its defenders had reinforced the ruined medieval walls with many concrete bunkers and trenches hacked out of the rock. Bombed and shelled during the initial phase of the invasion, its capture was assigned to the elite mechanised infantry of *Sayeret Golani*. The castle was taken in one night. Working their way slowly up to the castle's walls, trenches were cleared by grenades and machine-gun fire. By dawn the last bunkers had finally been cleared.

Currently, Israel deploys three regular parachute brigades, the 202nd, 890th and 50th *Nahal* Brigades, as well as three reserve brigades. IDF paratroops wear the standard Israeli uniform with a maroon beret and silver parachute wings on the left breast. In combat the paras carry the Galil assault rifle, which has replaced the venerable Uzi submachine gun as the airborne forces' individual weapon.

parachute brigades, while *Sayeret Golani* and *Sayeret Shimshon* serve the *Golani* and *Giva'ati* infantry brigades respectively. *Sayeret Hadruzim* is an elite Druze Muslim reconnaissance unit which is deployed on Israel's sensitive border with the Lebanon. Two other *Sayeret* units are involved in fighting terrorism. *Sayeret Shaldag* is the hostage-rescue unit and *Sayeret Mat'kal* is used for foreign operations.

Israel's most daring international operation was the rescue of the passengers of Air France Flight AF 139 in 1976. The Airbus aircraft was hijacked by Palestinian and Baader-Meinhof terrorists on 27 June and flown to Entebbe airport, Uganda. Once on the ground, the hostages were guarded by terrorists and Ugandan

US ARMY RANGERS

Since they were first formed in 1756, the Rangers have served with distinction in World War II, Korea, Vietnam, Grenada and Panama, often suffering heavy casualties. They are the US Army's expert recce troops.

ISOLATED, surrounded and almost defeated, Britain raised its commando forces in the dark days of 1940 to continue the struggle against Nazi Germany with small-scale raiding operations, even though Britain itself was still very much on the defensive strategically. This idea appealed to Brigadier Lucien K. Truscott Jr., attached to Combined Operations in the wake of America's entry in World War II following Pearl Harbor (7 December 1941). Although deeply suspicious of elite units, the US Army decided to raise similar formations and named them after an historical backwoods unit, Rogers' Rangers, active in the mid-eighteenth century. The officer chosen to lead the 'new' Rangers was Major William Darby, who took his recruits from all branches of the US Army. The lucky 500 who survived the two-week selection course of speed marches (the Rangers were to establish a US Army record by completing a 24km speed march in two hours) and assault courses, held at the unit's camp at Carrickfergus, Northern Ireland, went on to further training as the 1st Ranger Battalion. Throughout the war the 1st, and subsequent battalions, would be known, unofficially, as 'Darby's Rangers'.

At the Achnacarry Commando School in Scotland, the Rangers underwent more intensive training and selection before joining Combined Operations. Within months the

A Ranger on exercise in Germany. He is carrying a 5.56mm Minimi light machine gun, called the M249 Squad Automatic Weapon in the US Army. Note bipod tucked under the barrel.

1st Battalion saw action as assault troops supporting the Anglo-American 'Torch' landings in north Africa. On the night of 7/8 November 1942, Bill Darby led his men onto the beaches to clear two forts at the approaches to Oran harbour in Algeria. Even the French Foreign Legion forces of the Vichy French were no match for naval gunfire and the determined American commandos.

Over the next few minutes, more than 100 Italians were killed

From assault landings, the Rangers turned to raiding. Their first target was the Italian position at the Sened Pass, which called for a 32km forced march across the arid desert and a complicated battalion attack. The Rangers trekked across the stony desert by night and laid up by day to avoid enemy reconnaissance forces. After killing an enemy patrol at the foot of the mountains, the Rangers moved into position for a frontal assault. At the last moment, an enemy machine gun opened fire and the last 50m was covered in the face of cannon fire and flickering tracer. Over the next few minutes, more than 100 Italians were killed in a brutal battle fought with M1 Thompson submachine guns, grenades and fighting knives. Two months later, on 21 March 1943, Darby's raiders conducted a similar operation at El Guettar to clear Italian positions blocking General Patton's line of advance. The heavily defended positions were taken at dawn by men with blackened faces who gave shrill Red Indian war cries as they climbed down an escarpment to take the entrenchment from the rear. The enemy nicknamed the Rangers the 'Black Death' and a fighting legend was born.

In the battles for Sicily and Italy, the 1st Battalion was joined by the 3rd and 4th Rangers. On the offensive, the Allies used both the commandos and Rangers to spearhead landings, wresting heavily defended strongpoints from their defenders and blunting the inevitable German counterattacks. After Salerno (September 1943), the Rangers held the line in the mountains of the Venafro valley for 45 days, suffering 40 per cent casualties. At Anzio (January 1944), the three battalions splashed ashore on the bitterly cold morning of the 22nd to take the initial objectives. When Kesselring's units arrived to push the Allies back into the sea, the contest degenerated into bloody trench warfare reminiscent of World War I. On 25 January, in wet, muddy trenches around the Carroceto salient, the US Rangers repelled the Germans in four days of bloody fighting. On the 29th they were relieved, but only to march through the night to spearhead the US 3rd

Below: The 'Torch' landings in north Africa, November 1942. Here, Rangers of the 1st Battalion come ashore at Arzew in Algeria.

Division's attack on Cisterna, where the Ranger's 1st and 3rd Battalions suffered more than 60 per cent casualties. Some survivors were sent home to raise the famous North American Special Service Force. The 4th Rangers, with more than 180 casualties and five company commanders killed, was disbanded.

Rocket-fired grappling hooks and light assault ladders were to be used

Heroism and sacrifice had ensured the success of the Ranger concept. In April 1943, the 2nd Ranger Battalion, formed in the United States, was sent to Britain for training in cliff assault techniques. On D-Day (6 June 1944), three companies of the battalion won renown when they stormed the cliffs at Pointe du Hoc on the Normandy coast to destroy a battery of 155mm guns which had a clear field of fire onto the 'Omaha' and 'Utah' Beaches. The Rangers were given just 30 minutes to complete their mission

Above: Rangers training in Scotland, just prior to D-Day, for their cliff assault on the Pointe du Hoc.

before the first wave of infantry landed. Rough seas and enemy fire hampered attempts to reach the small strip of shingle below the enemy positions. Rocket-fired grappling hooks and light assault ladders were to be used to scale the steep cliff face, but when the Rangers finally reached the designated strip of beach, they found that a great many of the rockets had become waterlogged and the cliff was heavily defended. More than half of the three Ranger companies became casualties before the crest was reached. On the top they found a single artillery piece which had already been destroyed by naval gun fire.

Determined to find the missing battery, Lieutenant-Colonel Rudder, their commander, established a command post at the Pointe and then sent out fighting patrols towards their secondary objectives. The German guns were finally discovered sheltering from the naval gunfire in a small wood near the main road running behind the beach. After a brief but savage battle the battery was destroyed, but not before the patrols found themselves cut off from the Pointe by German units. Supported by naval gunfire, the survivors fought off numerous German counterattacks, while managing to slip fighting patrols through the lines to destroy an enemy ammunition dump and observation post. When they were finally relieved by the 116th Infantry Regiment on D+2, the three companies had each been reduced to around 20-man exhausted sections. That relief arrived when it did owed something to the remaining two companies of the 2nd Battalion and their sister unit, the 5th Rangers. Landing amongst the chaos and confusion of 'Omaha's' bloody Dog Green Beach, the Rangers led the 116th Infantry through the German defences, following General Norman Cota's now immortal command 'Rangers, lead the way.'

The Rangers killed 200 enemy soldiers for the loss of two killed

An equally famous Ranger unit was formed from the 98th Field Artillery Battalion in New Guinea on 20 August 1944. The 6th Ranger Battalion spearheaded the American drive into the Philippines and conducted two special operations that made it famous. The first was the daring rescue of American prisoners of war (POWs) from a Japanese camp on Luzon as, with the end of the war in sight, it was feared that the Japanese might start slaughtering their Allied prisoners. On 30 January 1945, a reinforced company of Rangers under Colonel Henry Mucci, with local guerrillas, attacked the camp at Cabanatuan. Although surrounded by two brigades of retreating enemy troops, Mucci used bullock carts to evacuate over 500 POWs through 40km of occupied territory. In the subsequent Japanese counterattacks, the Rangers killed 200 enemy soldiers for the loss of two killed and 10 wounded. In recognition of this extraordinary feat every soldier on the operation received a battlefield decoration.

The second operation occurred in June, at the end of the fighting on Luzon. Remnants of the once proud Japanese Army still held the northeast of the island and were fighting desperately in the hope of being evacuated through the port of Aparri. In order to bring this long, bitter campaign to an end, the Americans decided to block this last escape route by dropping a battalion of the 11th Airborne Division to capture the port. As there was little good intelligence on Japanese defences around the potential dropping zones (DZs), the 6th Rangers was ordered to act as pathfinders — laying out the DZs and holding them until the paratroops arrived. In what would later become a central task of the modern Rangers, B Company sneaked past the frontline units and carefully made its way through 400km of jungle on a 28-day reconnaissance mission. Finally, on 23 June, the Rangers selected a DZ and dug in around it. At 0900 hours the first aircraft appeared overhead. The wind speed was still very high but the paras jumped anyway, accepting the inevitable casualties as soldiers were blown into the trees. The landing was unopposed and the port fell quickly — three days later Japanese resistance ended.

As World War II came to a close the last Ranger units were deactivated, and it took another war in the Far East for the US Army to recognise the need for similar elite forces. When the North Korean People's Army (KPA) and their many Chinese 'advisors' invaded the Republic of Korea (ROK), the Allies, under a United Nation's mandate, responded quickly. In late June, seven KPA infantry divisions and an armoured brigade had crossed the border and, by the beginning of August, US and ROK forces had been pushed back into the south of the Korean peninsula around Pusan. At the eleventh hour the situation was brilliantly retrieved by General MacArthur, who reinforced the Allied perimeter at Pusan while also landing US troops at Inchon in the north to cut the communist forces in half. Over the next six months most of North Korea was overrun, only to be lost again when 180,000 Chinese troops swarmed across the Yulu River. With them came KPA commandos to fight a covert war behind American lines with propaganda, sabotage and assassination.

The US Army therefore looked for its own commando forces. As it was believed that operations deep behind the communist lines could only be executed by orientals, 20,000 ROK soldiers and North Korean defectors were organised into the United Nation's Partisan Forces in Korea. Raids and other elite duties in support of the US forces went to the reactivated Ranger companies. The Ranger Training Center (Airborne) at Fort Benning, Georgia, was created to train the first companies. By January 1951, eight companies had completed the

four-week cold weather course at Camp Carson, Colorado, and the 1st, 2nd, 3rd, 4th, 5th and 7th were sent to Korea.

The Rangers of the 2nd and 4th Companies were attached to the 187th Regimental Combat Team (RCT) — a 3500-strong independent airborne brigade. Landing craft and ships had been replaced by parachutes as a means of going into battle. Their first major operation with the RCT was at Munsan-ni in March 1951. Parachuting behind KPA lines, the Americans planned to cut off the PKA 19th Division as it attempted to retreat from an armoured onslaught. The Rangers' objective was the town of Munsan-ni itself which, in the

Below: Men of the 2nd Ranger Battalion board landing craft prior to Operation 'Overlord'.

best traditions of the Rangers, was taken and held despite relatively heavy casualties.

The other Ranger companies were attached to the US Eighth Army and assigned to various divisions and corps for elite infantry duties. Although often misused as an elite force that could be thrown into battle to hold 'lost' positions or spearhead counterattacks, the Rangers also conducted reconnaissance patrols, raids and ambushes befitting elite infantry. As the fighting in Korea ended, the Rangers were again deactivated. Only the Ranger School at Fort Benning remained.

Many units raised their LRRP platoons from Ranger School graduates

The American military reasoned that the advanced leadership course provided by the School would ensure that the infantry skills of the Rangers would percolate throughout the entire US Army — a particularly persuasive and cost-effective philosophy for the smaller peacetime Army. It was also proudly maintained that the US Army had never been defeated and was an elite formation in its own right — it had no need of special sub-units. Reluctantly, the military had allowed a small cadre of Special Forces ('Green Berets') to be raised. Although in theory they were trained in all aspects of guerrilla warfare and commando operations, the 'Berets' specialised in helping indigenous troops fight for themselves. In a major conflict requiring elite skills, there would in fact be too few Special Forces to support US fighting units. But nobody could conceive of such a conflict and all eyes were on Europe, where NATO faced the massive Soviet Red Army. Then, in the mid-1960s, an almost unknown Southeast Asian country began to suck the US Army into a modern guerrilla war: Vietnam.

The biggest problem facing the US Army in Vietnam was actually finding a very elusive enemy who refused to be drawn into combat. In the countryside the American soldier faced harassment from the local Viet Cong (VC)

Left: Rangers debuss from 'Huey' helicopters in Vietnam. As well as gathering intelligence, they undertook raids and ambushes against the VC.

guerrillas, who fought a shadow war to bring the hamlets and villages under communist control. Regular North Vietnamese Army (NVA) units entered South Vietnam via the Ho Chi Minh Trail — a network of roads and supply routes on the Laotian and Cambodian borders. All too frequently, an operation to sweep a VC-infested area turned into a pitched battle as the American troops encountered larger and more heavily armed units than expected. The key word was intelligence, and the primary means of gathering information was the long-range reconnaissance patrol (LRRP). Conducting 5-10 day patrols deep inside communist-held areas called for special skills and a certain type of man. Not surprisingly, many combat units raised their LRRP platoons from Ranger School graduates.

Ranger School tested a man's endurance, aggressiveness and confidence, and acted as a filter that retained the self-sufficient who could provide leadership under the most arduous and very dangerous conditions. The Ranger was also expected to be ready to fight in the jungles, mountains or icy wastes of the tundra as regular infantry, or in small groups behind enemy lines. He was trained in cliff assaults, survival, patrolling, unarmed combat, demolitions and escape and evasion. However, once selected for LRRP missions in Vietnam, Ranger School graduates faced further training. The Military Assistance Command, Vietnam (MACV) Recondo School provided a three-week course in patrolling run by instructors from the Special Forces. Once in the Vietnamese jungles and mountains, a patrol was usually forced to navigate with an error of less than half a kilometre. Troops were also schooled in the vital standing operational procedures for insertion and extraction and the complex signals arrangements for transmitting intelligence back to base, or calling in fire-missions and helicopter extractions to enable the team to escape from its pursuers.

Ninety per cent of the missions were carried out by 'light' reconnaissance patrols consisting of five or six men. Raids, prisoner snatches and the rescue of downed aircrew were conducted by 'heavy' patrols (most carried an M60 machine gun) of 6-10 men. The communist Special Forces mounted their own scout

Above: Rangers in Grenada, 1983. Both the 1st
and 2nd Battalions were involved in the invasion.

patrols to eliminate the LRRPs. Once an American patrol was discovered it was followed to determine its mission, then the patrol was marked for destruction. In August 1967, a reconnaissance patrol of the 173rd Airborne Brigade was operating close to the Ho Chi Minh Trail on the Cambodian border, when the tracker of a VC scout patrol picked up their trail. The five Americans had just taken a rest close to an old hill-top bunker complex, when they heard a distant shot to their front. As the patrol moved to take up defensive positions, a VC ambush was sprung from the jungle behind them. Two Americans were seriously wounded by the first volley of rifle fire and grenades. Returning fire, the Americans scattered down into the valley below. As the signaller fought to get out of the battle area, his radio antennae got snagged on a bush. With the enemy closing in around him, the radioman dropped his set and fled with the others.

In desperation, the patrol popped a yellow smoke grenade

The LRRP quickly re-grouped on the valley floor, but they were in big trouble. The nearest friendly forces were at Dak To Special Forces base, more than 20km away, and the patrol now lacked the means to request extraction. The patrol commander, Sergeant Charles J. Holland, estimated that there were more than 20 VC tracking his patrol. Grabbing some spare

clips of ammunition and a few grenades, he left his men and made his way back up the hill to provide a distraction and to recover the missing radio. Meanwhile, the unit commander, aware that Holland's patrol was off the net and that other LRRPs were reporting a firefight in the patrol's last location, ordered the team's emergency extraction.

High above the trees, the commanding officer's helicopter scoured the area for signs of his missing men. For over 45 minutes the patrol tried to attract the attention of the pilot with signal mirrors and red marker panels that signified that the patrol was still in contact with the enemy. Up on the hill, Sergeant Holland's firefight had suddenly gone quiet. In desperation, the patrol popped a yellow smoke grenade. Within minutes a helicopter touched down 50m away and the patrol was rescued under welcome covering fire from helicopter gunships. Sergeant Holland's dead body was later discovered surrounded by the patrol's equipment, he had been killed in hand-to-hand combat as he attempted to carry it down the hill. Holland was awarded the Distinguished Service Cross — the US Army's second highest award for gallantry.

In August 1967, the LRRP platoons were upgraded into companies but, with the 365-day rotation cycle, the reconnaissance units still suffered from the lack of an experienced permanent command structure. In January 1969, the 13 LRRP companies were given the title 'Ranger', designated C-I or K-P with the 75th Infantry Regiment as their parent unit. The World War II Ranger traditions had already been adopted by the US Army's Special Forces, while the 75th Infantry's history included 'Merrill's Marauders' — the American long-range penetration unit that had operated with the British Chindits in Burma. Although the Ranger companies now shared a common lineage, they remained under the command of the various units to which they were attached. It was only after the withdrawal from Southeast Asia that the Rangers were reactivated as the 1st Battalion (Ranger), 75th Regiment. A second battalion was raised on 1 October 1974, to be joined by a third in 1984, after the Rangers' outstanding performance in Grenada. The 75th Ranger Regiment is currently a component of the US Army Special Operation's Command (USASOC), itself a part of the joint service's United States Special Operations Command (USSOCOM).

Each Ranger battalion consists of a headquarters, headquarters company and three rifle companies, each of three platoons, and a support platoon — a total of 38 officers, two warrant officers and 571 men. The distinctive black beret and silver Rangers badge is worn by the battalions. All Ranger School graduates are entitled to wear the 'Ranger' shoulder flash. When not undergoing special-theatre training, the Rangers wear standard US Army uniform and remain the most lightly armed unit in the Army. The support platoons are equipped with mortars and anti-tank launchers. Each squad has one 40mm M203 grenade launcher and one Squad Automatic Weapon (SAW), which is com-patible with the standard M16A2 assault rifle and is a replacement for the M60 machine gun. Radio operators and some non-commissioned officers are issued with the far shorter CAR-15 submachine gun. Foreign weapons and ad-vanced automatic weapons (MP5 submachine gun and G-3 rifle) are on hand for special operations, but on recent missions in Grenada and Panama the Rangers depended upon rapid reinforcement by the more heavily equipped 82nd Airborne Division.

Below: On exercise in Panama. Stamina and self-discipline are the hallmarks of Ranger training.

THE FRENCH FOREIGN LEGION

Originally a motley collection of criminals, beggars, subversives and adventurers, the Foreign Legion is today a well-armed, crack fighting force. Disciplined, highly trained and motivated, the Legion is France's spearhead.

THE French Foreign Legion was created in an attempt to rid France of those unemployed officers and soldiers who were thought to be a threat to the reign of Louis-Philippe, who had come to power following the revolution of July 1830. The Legion was created by royal ordinance in March 1831 and officially only foreigners between the ages of 18 and 40 years were permitted to enlist. Officers were almost exclusively French, many of them veterans of Napoleon's *Grande Armée*. In reality, the Legion took what it could get and the poor and felons alike left workhouses and prisons to join its ranks. Dressed in ragged uniforms, both young and old were loaded onto ships for the arduous journey to Algeria. Once in the French colony, they were used as a labour corps and put to work building and repairing roads. Rarely has an elite unit been born in such humble circumstances.

Operation 'Desert Storm', February 1991. French 155mm artillery opens up on Iraqi positions to cover the Foreign Legion's advance during the liberation of Kuwait.

Above: A Legion patrol prior to a night reconnaissance of enemy positions around Bir Hakeim.

There was no shortage of recruits and the Legion quickly raised seven battalions. The 1st, 2nd and 3rd Battalions were composed mainly of Swiss and Frenchmen and were based in Algiers. The 4th Battalion was largely Spanish (Oran), whilst the 5th was composed mainly of Italians and Sardinians, and both battalions were stationed at Algiers. Dutch and Belgium nationals were recruited for the 6th Battalion (Bone) and Poles made up the 7th Battalion, although this replaced the 4th when Spain asked for the return of its citizens.

Initially, the Legion was tasked with the back-breaking work of general construction and road building — an unfortunate consequence of its ill-discipline and the general animosity and suspicion directed toward it by the high command of the French Army. However, the Legion did manage to see some action while supporting French operations and, much to the surprise of it's superiors, acquitted itself well. On 27 April 1832, the 1st and 3rd Battalions successfully stormed a stronghold of the troublesome El Ouffia tribe and, in November of that year, the 4th Battalion fought alongside regular French infantry, defeating the Emir of Mascara, Abd-el-Kader, on the slopes of the Djebel Tafaraouini, before the gates of Oran.

Two incidents in particular exemplify the unique spirit of the Legion. In early 1863, the Foreign Legion found itself in Mexico supporting the puppet government of the Emperor Maximilian. On 29 April of that year, a company of 63 legionnaires under the command of a Captain Danjou escorting a shipment of gold bullion were attacked by over 2000 Mexican rebels at the deserted hamlet of Camerone.

In the early hours of the morning the legionnaires were initially attacked by a force of cavalry, which they repulsed with some ease. However, in the general confusion of battle the mules carrying their water and ammunition had bolted, leaving them with only the supplies they were carrying. Danjou ordered a retreat to the deserted farmhouse and the legionnaires patiently awaited the next onslaught. Though he had lost 16 men killed in the first action, leaving him with only 47 men under his command, Danjou had confidence in his men's discipline and marksmanship. After a half-hearted attack

Right: Legionnaires on parade wearing the famous white *képis*, red epaulettes and blue sashes.

**Above: Fighting the Viet Minh in Indo-China.
Two German legionnaires engage enemy targets.**

on the farmhouse, the Mexicans, under a flag of truce, offered the legionnaires honourable surrender terms. These were curtly rejected and Danjou extracted a promise from each man that he would fight to the death. The Mexicans renewed their attack and were met by a hail of rifle fire; at around 1100 hours Danjou himself was killed. At noon the Mexicans were reinforced by a further 1000 infantrymen; by 1700 hours there were only 11 legionnaires left alive. An hour later there were only six legionnaires left standing, and they were without ammunition. After fixing bayonets they charged the Mexican positions, to be met by a hail of bullets which felled three of them and halted the rest. A Mexican colonel stepped forward and demanded their surrender. They replied that they would do so only if they were allowed to keep their arms and tend their wounded. He replied, 'one can refuse nothing to men like you.'

The second incident occurred in late 1918, when French and British forces intervened in the Russian civil war on the side of the 'Whites' — a loose grouping of Tsarist soldiers and general enemies of the Bolsheviks. Three Foreign Legion rifle companies and a machine gun company were raised in northern Russia, where they took part in the fighting around Archangel. Although the units were disbanded after the Allies withdrew, the locals, still in French uniforms, continued fighting until the 'White' Russians were finally crushed by the Red Army. Then, these ragged survivors from the French force made their way to the Legion's headquarters at Sidi-bel-Abbès, Algeria, to rejoin the only home left to them. These feelings can be found in the song of the 3rd REI, which includes the line 'My Regiment, My Homeland'.

By the end of World War I, the Legion had established itself as an excellent fighting unit, composed of men who were sometimes recklessly brave on the battlefield. As mentioned above, the Legion had originally been held in contempt and mistrust by the hierarchy of the French Army. As a result, the Legion developed a strong sense of self-reliance, an identity which gave rise to the concept of the Legion 'family'. Added to this was the harsh discipline that had been imposed as a result of the ill-discipline of its early period. Some 80 years after its formation, the Legion had developed from a ragtag rabble to a crack fighting force.

Other units fought the Germans in France before returning to Africa

World War II was a very troubled time for the Legion. In June 1940, the 13th Foreign Legion (Mountain) Half-Brigade (the 13th DBLE) was fighting in Norway when France fell to the German Army. Eventually repatriated with the rest of the Allied force to Britain, the legionnaires were given the opportunity of joining General de Gaulle and the Free French Forces, which many did. Other units fought the Germans in France before returning to north Africa to join the balance of the Legion under Vichy control. Altogether, around 2000 German legionnaires were rounded up by the German Army's inspectorate and press-ganged into their famous *Afrika Korps*. Worse was to follow when the 13th DBLE was sent to Syria, on the understanding that the Vichy forces were about to change sides. The rumour proved false and the 13th DBLE found itself in action against the Vichy 6th Foreign Infantry Regiment (the 6th REI), which was tasked with defending Damascus. Defeated, the Vichy forces surrendered on 14 July 1941. Two officers and a thousand legionnaires joined the 13th DBLE; the rest were eventually repatriated back to France and from there to Sidi-bel-Abbès. The 13th DBLE was posted to Egypt in December 1941; six months later it fought an heroic action defending the fortified position at Bir Hakeim against Rommel's attacks. For 14 days the legionnaires held out until ordered to break out on the night of 10/11 June. The Allied landings in French North Africa (Operation 'Torch') in November 1942 finally united most, but not all, of the Legion under Allied command.

In the Far East the Legion units in French Indo-China, including 5th REI, had, under orders from the Vichy Government, maintained an uneasy peace with their Japanese occupiers. Towards the very end of the war, Allied special services teams were parachuted into the region to orchestrate resistance against the Japanese. American Office of Strategic Services (OSS) officers jumped into both Vietnam and Laos to arm and train the local Viet Minh guerrillas, who were attracted by a promise of post-war independence. French 'Action Groups' made contact with the French generals and successfully persuaded them to change their allegiance and mount a quick coup against the Japanese. However, it was the Japanese who struck first. On the evening of 9 March 1945, the officers of the unsuspecting Lang Son garrison walked into a trap when they attended a banquet held in their honour. Those who refused to surrender were killed out of hand. Elsewhere, there was butchery as hordes of Japanese soldiers charged through the streets killing civilians. General Lemonnier and the French resident, Camille Auphalle, were beheaded when they refused to sign a surrender document.

An escalating cycle of violence resulted in the Legion invading the north

A column of the 5th REI, on operations near the Red River, made a fighting retreat towards the Chinese border. Crossing into Yunnan Province on 2 May 1945, the Legion left Indo-China for the first time in over 60 years.

At Potsdam (July 1945) the Allies divided Vietnam into spheres of influence: north of the Sixteenth Parallel was assigned to Chinese influence; south of it to Lord Louis Mountbatten's Southeast Asia Command, which was dominated by the British. In September, a Vietnamese Republic was proclaimed in the north under the leadership of Ho Chi Minh. The French, wishing to reassert their control over Indo-China, started negotiations with Ho for the establishment of an Indo-Chinese federation, excluding Saigon, which would be ruled directly from Paris. The Britsh handed over control to the French in October; in March 1946 an 'Accord' was signed between Ho and

the French government. Under this agreement France recognised the Vietnamese Republic and the Vietnamese in turn agreed to respect French interests — France was also allowed to base troops in the north. The uneasy peace lasted until November, when an escalating cycle of violence eventually resulted in the Legion invading the north.

The 2nd REI lost 230 men in three months of operations alone

The French attempted to hold Indo-China the same way they had pacified north Africa: by dominating the area with thousands of forts. At first the level of guerrilla activity was small, a consequence of the Viet Minh's poor organisation. However, in the follow-up operations the French lost heavily — the 2nd REI lost 230 men killed or wounded in three months of operations alone. The 1st and 2nd Foreign Parachute Battalions (the 1st and 2nd BEP) were raised in Algeriaa and sent to join the 2nd and 3rd REI and the 13th DBLE in Vietnam.

Left: Dien Bien Phu, March 1954. Legionnaires parachute in to reinforce the besieged garrison. Their efforts, however, would be to no avail.

Above: Legion paras counterattack against the Viet Minh at the Na San camp in November 1952.

A new phase of the war saw concentrated attacks against the French outposts. On 25 July 1948, 104 legionnaires of the 3rd REI were attacked at Phu Tong Hoa in the remote Cao Bang mountains. After bombarding the fort with mortars and artillery, the 316th Viet Minh Division launched human-wave attacks on three sides of the fort, flooding into the fort through a breach in the wall. The gap was only held by a lone legionnaire, Sergeant Huegen, armed with a light machine gun; reinforcements who joined him were killed in the fighting. By 2200 hours Huegen was dead, but the courtyard was again cleared with a bayonet charge. As the remaining legionnaires prepared for the next savage onslaught the clouds parted, illuminating the fort with bright moonlight. Unable to approach the fort unseen, the Vietnamese, their force decimated, withdrew into the night.

The French responded to this change of tactics by despatching an expeditionary force of 100,000 regular and provincial troops to Indo-China. The Legion was also reinforced by the 5th REI and by Legion units raised locally, but this did not prevent the post at Dong Khe

being decimated by six of General Giap's regular divisions on 17 September 1950. A greater disaster awaited the French at the Viet Minh's next target: the Legion fort at Cao Bang. The French high command decided on a dubious 'evacuation with honour', rejecting an airlift and condemning the garrison and 2000 civilian refugees to a nightmare 80km journey through mountainous jungle controlled by the enemy. A relief column called the Bayard Group, consisting of African troops strengthened by the 1st BEP, was promptly sent out to link up with the retreating garrison.

Throughout 1951 and 1952 almost all the Viet Minh offensives were defeated

The Bayard Group was soon in trouble, the column being split into small groups by repeated enemy attacks and finally trapped in the Coc Xa gorge. The nightmare descent into the gorge along a narrow mountainous trail cost the lives of over 100 legionnaires. The wounded were isolated and killed and the column was constantly harassed by snipers and so-called 'suicide commandos', who dragged the legionnaires off the narrow ledges that criss-crossed the sheer rock face 100m above the river. Only

Above: The Algerian War. A column from 1st REC on patrol near the Tunisian border in 1958. The Legion lost a total of 1900 killed in this conflict.

a small handful of survivors managed to reach the French-held city of Lang Son.

After the Cao Bang disaster the French appointed a new Commander-in-Chief, Jean de Lattre de Tassigny, who devised a strategy whereby the French would erect fortified camps on hostile territory before the enemy had chance to respond. This prompted the Viet Minh into attacking these positions, with corresponding losses. Throughout 1951 and 1952 almost all the Viet Minh offensives were defeated. In May 1953 Henri Navarre replaced Tassigny. He switched tactics to supporting remote bases with airstrips so that the garrisons could be reinforced more rapidly.

In November 1953, paras of the 1st BEP were dropped into the valley of Dien Bien Phu to reinforce a Legion fort on the Vietnamese-Laotian border. The aim of Operation 'Castor' was to build up forces for the French invasion of Laos and to relieve the pressure on the garrisons along the Red River delta. By merely occupying the Nam Yum River valley, the French deprived the communists of the annual

Above: Men from the 2nd REP on the ground at Kolwezi in May 1978. The speed of the Legion's assault was responsible for saving many lives.

2000-ton rice harvest and a large opium crop. The French base appeared to be impregnable. The major bastion and airstrip were protected by a series of heavily defended strongpoints code-named *Huguette*, *Dominique*, *Éliane*, *Françoise* and *Claudine*. Other isolated, heavily fortified outposts dominated either end of the valley — *Gabrielle*, *Béatrice*, *Ann-Marie* and *Isabelle*. These bunkers were specifically built to withstand ground assaults, and in the remote jungle heavy artillery strikes seemed inconceivable. By March 1954, the isolated base was garrisoned by over 16,000 men, 5000 of them legionnaires of the 1st BEP and two battalions of the 3rd REI and 13th DBLE.

On 13 March, the legionnaires of the 13th DBLE holding *Béatrice* were placed on alert in anticipation of a Viet Minh attack. The attack which materialised at 1700 hours was expected to be only a nuisance raid but, unknown to the French, General Giap was in fact assembling three divisions together with heavy artillery in the hills above the base. Nine hours later, battered into submission by artillery fire, *Béatrice*

was finally overrun by human-wave assaults. At midday, a cease-fire enabled French Red Cross teams to collect the wounded from *Béatrice* — they found only eight survivors. Of the 750-man battalion, less than 200 made it back to French lines.

Despite being reinforced by the Vietnamese Colonial Paras, *Gabrielle* was attacked and overrun the next night in another heavy attack. At first the 5/7th Algerian Rifles beat off an eight-battalion assault, however the Viet Minh returned with a 75mm recoilless rifle which they used to destroy the surviving machine gun posts. When 100 legionnaires from the 1st BEP counterattacked behind three M-24 tanks, they were ruthlessly cut to pieces by the crossfire from a prepared ambush.

The war had cost the lives of 10,483 legionnaires

The Vietnamese then changed their tactics. Every night the communist trenches were dug closer to the French lines. The final assaults were always launched after thunderous artillery barrages had smashed the shallow French bunkers to pieces. The Viet Minh artillery was also used very effectively to isolate Dien Bien Phu from the outside world. By the end of March, artillery strikes had effectively closed the airstrip. Aircraft dropping supplies to the beleaguered garrison were forced to run the gauntlet of small-arms fire and shells. The Viet Minh gunners even managed to destroy two B-26 bombers flying at an altitude of 3000m. During April the garrison received only 23 of 60 aerial re-supply drops. Eight C-119 transports were shot down and another 47 damaged by enemy fire. With only a small area of the base remaining under French control, the garrison fell on 6 May. Two battalions of the 13th DBLE and 3rd REI, the 1/2nd REI and the 1st and 2nd Parachute Battalions had disappeared at Dien Bien Phu, and with them went France's ambitions of remaining in Indo-China. The war had cost the lives of 10,483 legionnaires. Another 6328 went into captivity, from which only 2567 returned.

Revolt was also smouldering in French Algeria, the home of the Legion. On the day that Dien Bien Phu fell, the Revolutionary Committee of United Action met to form the National Liberation Front (FLN). They also fixed the date for the start of the revolt: All Saints Day, 1 November 1954. Military action would be carried out by bands of guerrillas (*fellagha*), members of the Algerian National Liberation Army (ALN) — the military wing of the FLN. The ALN divided the country into six military districts, each controlled by a company of *fellagha*. All Saints Day passed with a few scattered incidents, but gradually attacks on police stations and French civilians led to retaliations by the white colonists — massacre followed massacre. An FLN-orchestrated riot killed over 70 Europeans and 52 pro-French Arabs at Philippeville on 20 August 1955. More than 2000 Muslims were killed in reprisal.

Eventually, the French responded by erecting 350km of electrified fences, minefields and bunkers along the Tunisian ('Guelma Line') and Moroccan ('Morice Line') borders. However, infiltrators still managed to cross, blowing gaps in the wire and minefields with bangalore torpedoes. Once across the defensive lines, the *fellagha* faced mounted patrols and night ambushes. Farther south in the desert, units such as the 2nd REC mounted vehicle patrols to intercept parties crossing the border. Deeper inland, every town and village had its garrison of French conscripts and every civilian in Algeria was issued with an identity card.

Violence had inevitably spread to the capital Algiers, which was racked by a series of FLN bombings and right-wing counter-terror that made the city almost ungovernable. The tough 10th Parachute Division was sent in to restore order, cordoning off the casbah and breaking the FLN network down, cell by cell. At the top of the FLN's organisation was Yacef Saadi and Ali la Pointe. Both managed to remain at liberty until Saadi was captured in an undercover operation in September 1957, and la Pointe was killed during counter-terrorist operations in the casbah two weeks later.

Units of paratroops and legionnaires hunted the various ALN

In the countryside, units of paratroops and legionnaires hunted the various ALN units and attempted to cut their supply lines that ran across the border into sanctuary areas inside Morocco and Tunisia. In 1958, around 1000 *fellagha* were regularly attacking towns and villages behind the 'Guelma Line'. Facing them was the 1st REP under the able command of Lieutenant-Colonel Pierre Jeanpierre, who had devised new counter-insurgency tactics for the Legion. Companies of legionnaires were lifted into guerrilla-held areas by means of Sikorsky S-58 and Boeing-Vertol H-21 ('flying banana') helicopters. Once contact was made, one unit would engage the 'fell' while the other section or company rapidly advanced line abreast, tossing grenades into the undergrowth. Guerrillas who survived the grenades and broke cover were mown down by the MAT-49 machine guns carried by individual legionnaires. On 29 May 1958, Jeanpierre, hero of the Legion, was killed when his helicopter was shot down on the Djebel Mermera, but the 1st REP continued to fight the 'Battle of Guelma' throughout 1958 and 1959.

The battle for Algeria was lost not on the battlefield, but by public opinion in mainland France. Photographs of women and children being herded into resettlement camps under the

Above: Chad, 1984. Legionnaires manning a Hotchkiss-Brandt 120mm mortar prepare to fire.

'Challe Plan' (General Challe was appointed Commander-in-Chief in Algeria in December 1958), indiscriminate air attacks, together with hot-pursuit operations targeting guerrilla bases inside Tunisia all weakened French resolve. General de Gaulle, the French President, had held talks with FLN leaders in 1960 concerning Algerian independence. In April 1961, fearing that Algeria would be betrayed by the French Government, the military commanders in the colony staged an attempted coup (the General's Putsch). The coup failed and, as a consequence of its involvement, the 1st REP was disbanded. Algerian independence heralded a new era for the Legion, it settled in mainland France.

However, over the last two decades, the story of the modern Legion has continued to be intertwined with events in Africa. In April 1969 Chad found itself under threat from two rebel movements. General de Gaulle responded to the request for assistance by despatching a

tactical headquarters and two rifle companies of the 2nd REP. The key to locating the guerrillas in the arid mountains and deserts of northern Chad was mobility and speed — two of the basic ingredients of Legion operations in Algeria. Therefore, the paras used helicopters for reconnaissance and to mount quick-response operations from their base at Fort Lamy, while on the ground motorised and cavalry patrols provided the cutting edge to their operations. Within months these tactics had paid dividends against an enemy that had sanctuary areas along the Libyan and Sudanese borders.

A contingent of 2nd REP conducted several search and destroy operations

In September 1969, the 2nd Company was airlifted to Faya-Largeau, where the Chadian Army had been attacked by a large force of rebels. Feeling relatively secure, the guerrillas withdrew towards the remote mountainous area of Tibesti. Several days later, the legionnaires caught up with two groups of guerrillas in the area of the Bodo oasis. One of the 12 captured guerrillas was the rebel chief for the northern provinces. A similar pursuit by helicopters and ground forces a month later accounted for 68 rebels killed or captured. In the last battles of this phase of French intervention, a reinforced contingent of the 2nd REP conducted several successful search and destroy operations, before relieving the Chadian garrison at Zouar and spearheading a drive into a rebel base at the Leclerc Pass on the Libyan border. A month later, in May 1970, a large force of rebels on the Sudanese border was cornered in caves in the area of Fada. These operations eliminated a combined total of around 130 guerrillas and destroyed much of the two rebel organisations.

France offered to mount a rescue and despatched the elite 2nd REP

The Foreign Legion returned to Chad in March 1978 to train and lead the Chadian Army against the rebel forces of Goukouni Oueddi, who was being supported by Libya's leader, Colonel Gadaffi. Having occupied most of northern parts of the country, rebel forces were reported as far south as the town of Ati. At l'Oued Batha, reconnaissance elements of the 2nd REP were confronted by rebel forces armed with artillery and a range of modern support weapons. However, they proved no match for the French Jaguar ground-attack aircraft, and the town was quickly retaken. France was again asked to intervene in Chad in August 1983, but Operation 'Manta' was notable only in the fact that rebel forces were frequently supported by the Libyan Air Force.

The 2nd REP saw two other significant operations in Africa. On 3 April 1976, the paratroops supported the successful GIGN rescue of French children from a terrorist-held bus on the Djibouti-Somalia border. Two years later, in May 1978, the Foreign Legion paratroops mounted their own airborne rescue, when Congolese rebels crossed into Zaire and seized the small mining town of Kolwezi. When it was learnt that the Katangan 'Tigers' were bent upon revenge and had began slaughtering Kolwezi's 2300 European inhabitants, France offered to mount a rescue and despatched the

elite 2nd REP — the audacious Operation 'Leopard' was under way.

Moving with incredible speed, the first contingent of legionnaire paratroops, 650 men headed by the regiment's commander, Colonel Erulin, landed northeast of the town at 1500 hours on 19 May, having left Corsica at 0800 hours on 18 May. After quickly eliminating resistance around the dropping zone (DZ), the legionnaires advanced towards the town itself. After heavy fighting Kolwezi fell to the paras, and the next day the regiment's 4th Company and Reconnaissance Platoon were parachuted in. The legionnaires then mounted an assault upon the native quarter of Marika, which proved to be a tougher nut to crack. In the vicious house-to-house fighting which ensued four legionnaires were killed, and the area was only secured after a heavy mortar barrage. Later that day the second echelon of 2nd REP, together with Belgian para-commandos, arrived, thus allowing the whole area around the town to be cleared. The operation had been a resounding success; for the loss of five dead and 25 wounded, the 2nd REP had saved the lives of hundreds of European civilians and had killed 250 guerrillas and captured a further 163.

The Daguet Division was asked to cover the left flank of the operation

More recently, the Foreign Legion made an important contribution to the 10,000-strong Daguet Division that took part in Operation 'Desert Storm'. The French force consisted of the 72 AMX-10 infantry fighting vehicles and mechanised infantry of the 6th Light Armoured Division, which included the 1st REC, 2nd REI and 6th REG, under the overall command of Lieutenant-General Michel Roquejeoffre.

Combined with the US 82nd Airborne Division, the Daguet Division was asked to cover the entire left flank of the operation. Driving deep into the desert behind a screen of Gazelle helicopters on 24 February, the two divisions contacted elements of the Iraqi Army in the

Legionnaires, including a Milan team, in the Saudi desert debuss from their VAB armoured personnel carrier during the Gulf War with Iraq.

area around Salman. In the resulting action the American paratroops provided flank protection screens, while the French, including the Legion regiments, overran and eliminated the Iraqi 45th Division. For the next two days, the Allied forces continued to push north to cut the vital Baghdad-Basra road at As Samawah on the River Euphrates, thus closing the most immediate escape route of the Iraqi forces retreating from Kuwait. This placed the Franco-American force a mere 240km from the Iraqi capital and in an excellent position, if the decision had been taken, to strike at Baghdad.

Currently, the Foreign Legion is composed of two administrative and training regiments (the 1st RE and 4th RE), three infantry regiments (the 2nd REI, 3rd REI and 5th REI), one half-brigade (the 13th DBLE), one armoured regiment (the 1st REC), one engineer regiment (the 6th REG) and a parachute regiment (the 2nd REP). In addition, there is the small *Detachment de Légion Etrangère de Mayotte* (DLEM), a former company of the 3rd REI which is based on the island of Mayotte.

Individual legionnaires are armed with the FA MAS 5.56mm assault rifle, the standard infantry weapon of the French Army. Capable of single shots and short bursts, this bullpup design rifle, which is fitted with a bipod, can also be adapted to fire anti-tank rounds. Other small arms include the 7.62mm light machine gun, several repeating rifles and the FR-F1 bolt-action rifle, which is issued to the sniper sections in each rifle platoon. The rifle is usually fitted with a telescopic sight for daylight use, with a night sight also available.

While the traditional headdress of the *képi blanc* (legionnaires) and the *képi noir* (NCOs and officers) is worn with 'walking out' dress, or on parades and other formal occasions, the green beret has been on general issue to the Legion since 1959. The standard Legion beret badge is the seven-flamed grenade. The paras of the 2nd REP wear the Legion beret with the hand and dagger emblem. Parachute wings are worn over the right tunic pocket. The Foreign Legion's motto is the apt *Legio Patria Nostra* — The Legion is our Homeland.

SPETSNAZ

Highly secretive and deadly, *spetsnaz* units were not even acknowledged to exist by the Soviet Union until recently. These crack troops are trained to undertake a wide variety of tasks including assassination, sabotage and disabling enemy nuclear weapons.

VOISKA *Spetsialnogo Naznacheniya* (VSN) — forces of special designation — have no real equivalent in the West. In the eyes of the Soviet Union they are forces of special designation rather than NATO-style commando units. Until 1989, references in the Soviet military press to VSN were rare and usually couched in historical terms. Reference to activities such as special reconnaissance (*spetsialnaya razvedka*) or diversionary reconnaissance (*diversiya razvedka*) appeared in the Soviet military press, but the existence of a multi-talented elite within the Soviet Army was discounted as Western propaganda.

This was partly a deliberate deception by the Soviets, but there are also conceptual differences between Western and Soviet Special Forces. The West was slow to accept the need for elite forces capable of carrying out special operations. When such troops were recognised, after their large-scale use in World War II, they tended to be packaged into elite units with their own highly specialised roles, training, selection and weaponry. In contrast, the USSR was eager to spread the ideology of communism and was quick to appreciate the value of special operations and resourceful, politically-reliable troops capable of operating independently in harsh climates and behind enemy lines. Consequently, the Soviets deploy a wider range of special operations-capable units, with the result that the *Vozdusho Desantniye Voiska* (VDV) airborne divisions, air assault

Following a successful raid against Mujahedeen positions in northern Afghanistan, near the Soviet border, *spetsnaz* troops return to a waiting Hip helicopter.

brigades, airborne naval infantry and the like are not seen in the West as bona fide special forces. Once behind enemy lines, the primary task of these units is to conduct mainly overt conventional operations at battalion or brigade strength.

The *spetsnaz* are different in being dedicated to one or more types of covert special operations and in receiving specialised training in intelligence gathering (*razvedchiki*), long-range reconnaissance patrols (*iskatelia*), abductions (*okhotniki*), foreign raids (*reydoviki*), partisan support, sabotage and assassinations. *Spetsnaz* units usually have a historical tradition of special operations and are controlled by the intelligence staff of a Fleet, Front, theatre or Army headquarters.

Cheka detachments saw considerable action during the civil war

The first recorded use of forces of special designation by the Soviets occurred soon after the Revolution. The Red Army was considered too politically unreliable to undertake operations against fellow workers and peasants. In the spring of 1918, the *Chasti Osobogo Naznacheniya* or ChON (detachments of special designation), comprising detachments of communist workers, were moved into the major industrial cities to ensure the civilian population's total adherence to the new regime. A year later the force was expanded by the All-Russian Extraordinary Commission to Combat Counter-Revolution and Sabotage (Cheka) — a predecessor of the KGB — into a paramilitary territorial unit within the Red Army. Cheka and ChON units were involved in crushing the Kronstadt uprising in March 1921, when Cheka machine gunners were placed in the rear of the Red Army forces to discourage desertion or retreat. Cheka detachments also saw action during the civil war and against the Islamic counter-revolutionaries or *basmachi* (bandits) in the southern Soviet Union.

The Soviets also pioneered the use of airborne special forces. Reconnaissance teams (*razvedchiki*), formed in 1927, were used against Afghan insurgents in 1929 and against the *basmachi* in Central Asia until the latter's virtual

Above: Her comrades resting, a lone partisan stands guard behind German lines in the Ukraine.

suppression in 1931. By 1932 the embryonic regular airborne forces had become almost completely dedicated to deep reconnaissance (*spetsialnaya razvedka*) and to the destruction of the enemy's command and control facilities.

By the early 1930s, Soviet special operations units had largely crushed the majority of domestic dissent and felt ready to concentrate on directing their attention against anti-Soviet activity abroad. In 1936 the Cheka created an Administration for Special Tasks to implement the ruthless elimination of its enemies abroad. During the Spanish Civil War (1936-39), for example, the newly formed *Narodnyy Komissariat Vnutrennikh Del* (People's Commissariat of Internal Affairs) — now the KGB — and *Glavnaye Razvedyvatelnoye Upravleniye* (Main Intelligence Directorate of the General Staff) undertook terrorist, sabotage and guerrilla activities behind Nationalist lines on a scale never before envisaged.

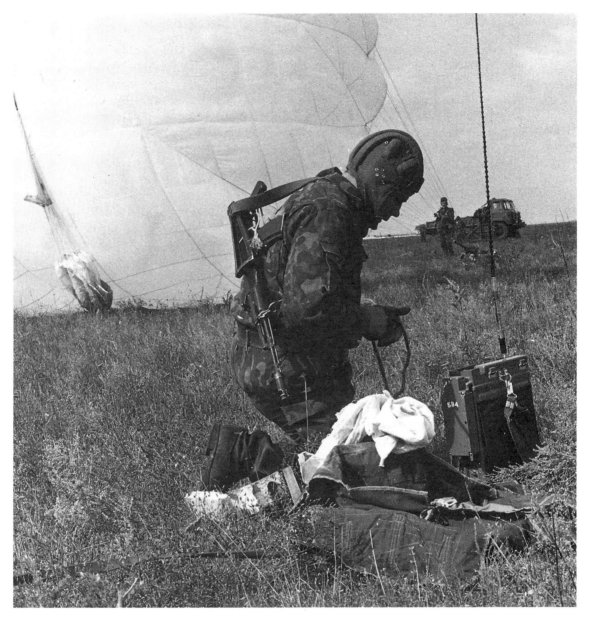

Above: Having just landed, a *spetsnaz* soldier checks his equipment. *Spetsnaz* recruits are selected for their intelligence and motivation.

During the early stages of the Great Patriotic War (1941-45), the Soviets created a wide variety of Chekist, GRU, assault combat engineer and naval special reconnaissance units. Few of these early conscript units were truly elite, but nevertheless they played a crucial part in the ultimate Soviet victory. Many more elite formations were created and given tasks that incorporated the lessons of the earlier airborne *razvedchiki* with the experiences of the Cheka agents. These were the reconnaissance-diversionary brigades, NKVD special groups, guards battalions and headquarters reconnaissance detachments — which can be considered as the true antecedents of the modern *spetsnaz*.

These forces fought on the Eastern Front, above the arctic circle in northern Russia, Finland and Norway, and in the Soviet Far East and Manchuria. In late 1941, in an attempt to gain intelligence on German strengths in the

119

Murmansk area, the Northern Fleet formed the 4th Special Volunteer Detachment of Sailors. Many of the recruits were accomplished linguists and the unit also employed Finnish and Norwegian agents who chose to fight with the Soviets. Ultimately renamed the 181st Special Reconnaissance Detachment (*osobogo razvedyvatel'nogo otriada*), this force was the ancestor of the modern naval *spetsnaz*. Tasked directly by Fleet Commander Admiral Golovko, the many agents and commandos of the Detachment often operated hundreds of kilometres from their home base at Poliarnyi. Whilst some undertook aggressive search and destroy missions against German shoreline installations, others undertook covert reconnaissance, target acquisition, coast and river watching, prisoner snatching and field interrogation.

By October 1942, every Front and Army Headquarters had been allotted a guards battalion of demolition experts called 'miners' —

Below: A *spetsnaz* patrol on exercise near the Norwegian border. Clandestine infiltration is a speciality of the Soviet Union's crack troops.

otdelnyy gvardeyeskiy batal'on minerov (OGBM). These troops were taught long-range reconnaissance patrolling skills, demolition and sabotage, terrain and night navigation, escape and evasion and the necessary skills to survive for long periods in the forests, swamps and tundra. As with all Soviet special purpose forces, OGBM troops were selected on the basis of their absolute loyalty to the Communist Party, resilience and stamina. Most were Party members, 18- to 30-years-old and, in many cases, were very experienced sportsmen and hunters. Standing operational procedures were relentless and nothing was allowed to interfere with the successful execution of an objective. Both in training and on operations, injured and exhausted soldiers were simply left to their own devices, a factor that contributed to their very high casualty rate.

Working closely with the various partisan groups, they either crossed the front line in small groups at night or were inserted by parachute, landing usually some 15km from their objective. The partisans provided the 'miners' with local intelligence, guides and security for

the demolition teams. In return, the 'miners' provided training in sabotage and target acquisition and replenished the partisans' stocks of explosives. Immediately before the large Soviet Smolensk offensive in July 1943, 316 'miners', in nine groups, were parachuted behind the Kalinin Front. Operating up to 300km behind the German's front line, the partisans and 'miners' laid more than 3500 charges on an aggregate length of 700km of railway track.

Small groups of special purpose forces were parachuted behind Japanese lines

On the night of 11 March 1943, a 23-man party from the 9th OGBM led by Lieutenant I.P. Kovalev parachuted behind German lines in the Novorzhev area of the Northwestern Front. After making contact with the 1st Partisan Regiment (3rd Partisan Brigade), the 'miners' went into action on 17 March, laying charges and delayed-action mines on local roads and railways. Over the next seven months, the group sabotaged 1500m of telephone lines, 8000m of railway track and 17 bridges. These actions resulted in the destruction of two tanks, eight truck loads of ammunition, several dozen vehicles and 16 military trains. In subsequent actions the 'miners' and partisans were credited with killing around 500 German troops. When the partisans and commandos linked up with the Red Army in October 1943, Kovalev was awarded the Hero of the Soviet Union, with the rest of the party receiving the Order of the Patriotic War or Red Star.

Above: In Afghanistan *spetsnaz* **troops were used as the spearhead of anti-guerrilla operations.**

During the winter of 1942-43, OGBM groups behind the lines derailed 576 trains and five armoured trains, blew up approximately 300 tanks and self-propelled guns, 650 wheeled vehicles and armoured cars and more than 300 rail and road bridges, killing and wounding thousands of enemy soldiers in the process. During the July 1943 fighting in the Kursk Salient, for example, the 1st Guards Engineer Brigade destroyed 140 tanks and self-propelled guns and inflicted 2500 German casualties. Over a two-year combat period, sabotage teams of the 13th OGBM were credited with destroying over 90 tanks, 11 self-propelled guns, 214 vehicles, nine trains and four bridges, killing more than 2000 enemy troops.

As the war in the East against Japan moved to its inevitable conclusion, the Soviets began to master the art of *maskirovka* (deception). Small groups of special purpose forces were parachuted behind Japanese lines in Manchuria to link up with well-armed groups of partisans in the last great Soviet offensive of the war. Once in position, they organised attacks against unsuspecting logistical centres as if to suggest that the area had been designated as a future major axis of advance. Enemy troops would be redeployed to the area to counter the threat only to discover, too late, that the attack was to be mounted in an entirely different sector many kilometres away. *Maskirovka* provided a lesson never to be forgotten by the Soviet forces and

121

one subsequently to be used to great effect by future *spetsnaz* elements. Immediately after World War II the USSR disbanded its forces of special designation, delegating diversionary operations to conventional airborne units. During the late 1950s, however, they reformed their specialist units, structuring them within the existing KGB and GRU frameworks.

Spetsnaz teams demolished the central military communications centre

Spetsnaz forces were an integral part of the Soviet operation to suppress the 'Prague Spring' in 1968. In order to mask their intentions towards Czechoslovakia for as long as possible, and being well versed in the art of *maskirovka*, the Soviets pointedly confined the vast majority of their troops within Group of Soviet Forces Germany (GSFG) to barracks immediately prior to the invasion. The Czechs had nothing to fear, therefore, when an unscheduled civilian Aeroflot aircraft landed at Prague's Ruzyne Airport late at night, taxied and parked at the end of the runway. An hour later a second Aeroflot aircraft landed. This aircraft disembarked its passengers who, having cleared customs, set off for the city centre. Two hours later the 'passengers', now fully armed, returned to take over the main airport buildings. Almost at once, one, or possibly two, further aircraft landed carrying teams of uniformed *spetsnaz*. This was the first in a series of transports containing *spetsnaz* and conventional troops of the 103rd Guards Airborne Division. Within two hours of the first uniformed *spetsnaz* troops landing, the airport and its environs were in Soviet hands and the capital was under overt attack. By day-break the presidential palace, the radio and television studios, the city's main transmitter, principal railway stations and the bridges over the River Vltava were all under Soviet control.

The role played by *spetsnaz* in the takeover of Afghanistan was no less critical. Between 8 and 10 December 1979, some 14 days before the invasion, *spetsnaz* troops, in the company of an airborne regiment, deployed to Bagram, a key town to the north of Kabul, to secure the Salang Highway with its critical tunnel.

Between 10 and 24 December, a battalion from the regiment, together with the *spetsnaz* contingent, moved to Kabul International Airport, less than three kilometres from the city centre. Between 24 and 27 December, troops from the 105th Guards Airborne Division, again supported by *spetsnaz*, landed at and secured Kabul Airport, together with the air force bases at Bagram, Shindand and Kandahar. During the course of the next night the full offensive began. Paratroopers arrested members of the Afghan government whilst *spetsnaz* teams demolished the central military communications centre. *Spetsnaz* teams also captured the still functioning Ministry of the Interior, the Kabul radio station and several other key points.

Simultaneously, two *spetsnaz* companies, with KGB assistance and supported by an airborne regiment, attacked President Amin's palace situated at Darulaman. Amin, his family, entourage and guards were killed in the subsequent battle. The Soviets lost 25 dead

Above: *Spetsnaz* forces do not have their own distinctive uniforms as such, but rather wear other units' gear. These two are wearing paratrooper kit.

including KGB Colonel Bayerenov, reportedly hit by 'friendly' crossfire. Soviet internal security troops may also have been present, possibly even 'units of special designation', as evidenced by the participation of Major-General V. S. Paputin of the MVD, apparently killed, like Colonel Bayerenov, during an abortive *spetsnaz* attempt to seize the palace before the main assault.

Spetsnaz units passed the first two years of the Afghan War quietly, defending their barracks and major installations. They were also used to defend the command structure in Kabul, while two *reydoviki* battalions are reported to have used aggressive patrolling to blunt guerrilla attacks against the airfields at Jalalabad and Kandahar.

Infiltration and supply routes were ambushed or peppered with mines

In 1983, however, *spetsnaz* forces went on the offensive. Working in conjunction with heli-borne troops and Afghan militia, they attacked isolated towns and villages which the Mujahedeen had once considered safe. These tactics are reported to have been used in November 1984 during fighting at Black Mountain in Nangarhar Province. Infiltration and supply routes were ambushed or peppered with mines, while villages suspected of helping the guerrillas were razed to the ground in a 'scorched earth' policy as vicious as any seen in Vietnam. Some of these operations may have been carried out by *spetsnaz* disguised as guerrillas, who burned mosques and food supplies to heighten tension between warring Mujahedeen factions.

In the spring of 1985 *spetsnaz* conscripts, drawn from the special operations brigades, began to operate in close conjunction with conventional ground troops in an attempt to rid the Afghan valleys of enemy activity. During

Left: In wartime *spetsnaz* troops would work closely with units such as the elite Guards Airborne divisions (seen here).

two well-publicised sweeps along the Kunar Valley, helicopter-inserted *spetsnaz* troops moved along the high ground far ahead of the advancing tanks and armoured personnel carriers (APCs) to catch the unsuspecting enemy in the open. Casualties on both sides were heavy but the Soviets appeared willing to pay this high price in order to reduce guerrilla attacks on road convoys. Similar tactics are reported to have been used to defend convoys, with *spetsnaz* piquets being inserted by helicopter ahead of the vehicles.

While the regimental *spetsnaz* troops continued to operate closely with the ground troops, the regular headquarters detachments were given almost complete autonomy. These troops, usually in their thirties, battle-hardened and totally acclimatised to mountain warfare, quickly began to register successes. Reconnaissance (*razvedka*) units would operate from camouflaged hides high in the mountains. The results of their reconnaissance and surveillance patrols were often encoded into high-speed

Morse and sent directly to the GRU for dissemination to the planners in the Kremlin. Some groups would be disguised as peasants to enable them to move comparatively freely about the mountain passes. Others were dropped many kilometres from their objective, travelling overnight to lay ambushes and observe infiltration routes. Depending on the tactical situation, mountain trails were mined, targeted for air strikes or ambushed. Some of these operations employed BMD airborne infantry fighting vehicles lifted in by helicopter. *Spetsnaz* activity within Afghanistan was curtailed when the Mujahedeen started to receive large shipments of American-made surface-to-air Stinger missiles. Nevertheless, the role of *spetsnaz* within the Afghan campaign remained significant until the final Soviet withdrawal.

The Special Operations Brigade — of which 16 existed at the height of the Cold War — is the basic *spetsnaz* unit. One brigade is assigned to each Military District, whose forces form an operational wartime Front. These are

Below: Two tense *spetsnaz* soldiers in a Hip helicopter during a raid against Mujahedeen positions around the besieged city of Barikot, June 1985.

Above: Fighting an internal enemy. An elite MVD hostage-rescue unit undergoing anti-terrorist drill.

subordinate to the Chief Intelligence Directorate (GRU) of the General Staff. In addition, each of the four fleets have a naval *spetsnaz* brigade subordinate to the Intelligence Directorate at Naval Headquarters. Each brigade usually comprises a headquarters element, a headquarters company, three or four parachute battalions and other supporting units. A *spetsnaz* brigade has between 1000 and 1300 men and is trained to operate either as a single unit or in a number of sub-units to a maximum of 135. It is highly trained in specialist assassination and subversion roles, liaises directly with *spetsnaz* field agents and, therefore, is likely to come under direct GRU operational control. It is also probable that it liaises directly with its opposite numbers within KGB *spetsnaz*. Although highly trained, these headquarter companies are relatively small.

Two more *spetsnaz* formations are tasked below district level. A *spetsnaz* regiment, comprising between 600 and 700 men divided into six or seven companies, is attached to each tactical theatre. Until recently, one regiment, based within the Non-Soviet Warsaw Pact (NSWP), was maintained in a constant state of readiness, but this has now been withdrawn to

the USSR. The 'Independent Company', one of which is attached to each Army, consists of a headquarters and three parachute platoons plus various logistics/communications support. Although the exact size will vary according to the nature of any specialist task allotted to it, company strength is always in the region of nine officers, 11 warrant officers and 95 men. While capable of operating as a single unit, each company will normally divide into 2-15 sub-modules. The structure of each sub-group is not rigid and may even change during the operation of a mission.

During the course of the recent Soviet domestic unrest it became clear that a new elite cadre has been added to the Interior Ministry troops (MVD), who are responsible for internal security. Photographs appearing in the publication *Novotni* have shown fit young MVD personnel carrying AKS-74 assault rifles with an extra magazine taped to the one inserted into the weapon. These troops were issued with conventional camouflage trousers and jackets but wore bright scarlet berets in the floppy

Above: An *Oznaz* team, known as the 'brotherhood', descends through the floor of an Mi-8 helicopter during counter-terrorism training.

style of the Soviet paratrooper. In action these troops wore equally distinctive white helmets.

It is probable that this MVD unit of special designation, variously referred to in the press as *Oznaz* or *Omon*, comprises the Soviet Union's latest anti-terrorism team. It is even possible that the group is geared to undertake hostage-rescue missions in conjunction with the KGB's own internal hostage-rescue unit (HRU). All are army veterans, mostly ex-paras with experience of combat in Afghanistan. A recent article in *Krasnaya Zvada* suggests that the unit is part of the elite Dzerzhinsky Division. Its members undergo a 10-month training programme at their own training centre in the Moscow area. The course starts with unarmed combat and fitness training before progressing to hostage-rescue scenarios employing aircraft and an SAS-style 'killing house'. This special designation company should not be confused with the MVD 'blue berets', which are regular MVD troops drafted into particularly volatile areas to support the local, often poorly trained and outnumbered, conscript forces.

The KGB *spetsnaz* is the most secretive and mysterious of all the Soviet units of special designation. While its more aggressive activities have been curtailed in the light of the recent Cold War thaw, KGB *spetsnaz* is known to focus on foreign strategic, social, economic and political targets. It consists of a small cadre of professionals assisted by several hundred support personnel, including clandestine agents. It may be assumed to have its 'legals' — accredited diplomats who often masquerade as commercial attaches — in most key embassies and may even run teams of 'illegals', i.e. citizens (not usually Soviets) living in the target country who are not covered by the protection of diplomatic status.

Organised within Department Eight, a tiny cell within Directorate S (Illegals), KGB *spetsnaz* conducts a small number of painstakingly selected operations under conditions of extreme security, e.g. strategic sabotage and assassinations. KGB *spetsnaz*, disguised as conventional airborne troops, accompanied their GRU and, possibly, MVD *spetsnaz* colleagues on the assault on Darulaman which resulted in the murder of President Amin and his entire family.

THE BRITISH SAS

The Special Air Service is the most highly trained special forces unit in the world. Since its formation in World War II, the Regiment has achieved some startling victories. Today, it is at the forefront of the fight against international terrorism.

THE most famous of the world's elite units was formed in somewhat unusual, if not curious, circumstances. The background to the Special Air Service (SAS) Regiment's creation was the bitter struggle in north Africa during World War II. Throughout 1941 the *Deutsches Afrika Korps*, commanded by General Erwin Rommel, had reversed early British successes and pushed the numerically stronger British Army back into Egypt. To stem the tide a way had to be found to strike at the vulnerable German rear areas. The founder of the SAS was a Scots Guards officer, David Stirling, who had arrived in the Mediterranean with 'Layforce', a group of five Commandos (Nos 7, 8, 11, 50 and 52) named after their commander, Brigadier Robert Laycock. After actions in Crete and Syria and several not always successful raids on the north African coast, Layforce went to Egypt, where it was disbanded in the summer of 1941. While a smaller force — Middle East Commando — remained attached to the Eighth Army, many of the men were returned to their original units.

A Royal Navy Sea King helicopter off-loads an SAS team during a winter warfare exercise in Norway. All Special Air Service soldiers are trained to operate in any type of terrain.

His unhappy experiences with Layforce convinced Stirling that large-scale commando-type amphibious raids on coastal installations frequently lost the element of surprise, and relied too heavily on the thinly spread resources of the Royal Navy. Stirling devised a plan to parachute small teams behind enemy lines which would simultaneously attack targets such as petrol dumps and airfields, thereby causing maximum damage to German supply lines. The deactivation of Layforce presented Stirling with an opportunity to present his views to the Deputy Chief of Staff, Major-General Neil Ritchie. Circumventing the traditional slow military channels, in his own words the 'fossilised shit', Stirling, still on crutches as the result of a parachuting injury, forced his way into Ritchie's office. The young lieutenant was lucky. Prime Minister Churchill had been urging the Commander-in-Chief Middle East, General Claude Auchinleck, to establish a guerrilla force that would compel the Germans to divert men and equipment away from their front line.

As his idea required few men and materials, Stirling's memorandum also satisfied the intelligence staff, who were desperately trying to convince the Germans that another parachute brigade had reinforced the British Eighth Army — the deliberately deceptive 'Special Air Service' title had already been applied to the initial cadre of the Parachute Regiment (11 SAS Battalion). Consequently, although Stirling, now promoted to the rank of captain, was given permission to raise 'L-Detachment' of the SAS Brigade, it was more officially known as the No 1 Small Scale Raiding Force. It was only in February 1943, after Stirling's soldiers had breathed life into the deception, that the unit became the 1st SAS Regiment.

Senior staff officers of the RAF and Eighth Army were suitably impressed

That the SAS became more than just another private army owed much to the fact that its new commander recruited a range of highly talented and skilled men from his former unit, No 11 (Guards) Commando. The names of 'Jock' Lewes, Bob Bennett, Johnny Cooper, Bob Lilly and Reg Seekings are renowned in the early

Above: The charismatic founder of the Special Air Service, Lieutenant-Colonel David Stirling.

history of the SAS. Eoin McGonigal, one of the first members of the unit, probably introduced Stirling to one of his most famous officer recruits, 'Paddy' Blair Mayne, who at the time was under arrest for delivering a knockout punch to the chin of his commanding officer during a rumpus in the mess.

The unit's first two 'raids' did much to ensure its immediate survival — both were against friendly targets. First, an impromptu sortie on a neighbouring New Zealand camp equipped the new force with the necessities of life. The second 'raid' resulted from a bet with a senior RAF officer and entailed a long and difficult forced march through the desert under constant aerial surveillance to attach stickers to Allied aircraft inside a heavily guarded RAF base. Senior staff officers of the RAF and Eighth Army were suitably impressed. Unfortunately, the first operation to hit German airfields west of Tobruk was a disaster. On the night of 18 November 1941, five aircraft carrying 64 men took off for their respective dropping zones (DZs) but soon ran into gale force winds and heavy rain. Two aircraft were lost and the parachutists widely scattered. As a consequence, no targets were attacked and, two days later, only 22 tired and hungry men struggled into the rendezvous (RV) with the Long Range Desert Group (LRDG).

After a meeting with the LRDG patrol commander, Captain David Lloyd-Owen, Stirling realised that the LRDG could provide transport both to and from the targets. Two weeks later the partnership was sealed and jeep-borne SAS parties raided four airfields. Despite finding that only two were operational, Stirling's men destroyed 61 aircraft and a number of vehicles. The raid was also notable for the fact that 'Paddy' Mayne destroyed a German aircraft with his bare hands. Later, Stirling walked into an LRDG RV without giving the password and the sentry opened fire at point-blank range; fortunately the round was a dud. Nevertheless, LRDG jeeps were clearly much safer than parachutes for getting SAS teams to their targets.

Once the SAS had learnt the art of desert patrolling from the LRDG, they mounted their own jeep patrols. By January 1943, David Stirling's SAS had managed to destroy over 250 aircraft and numerous vehicles in road ambushes, forcing the Germans to divert large numbers of troops and anti-SAS units to hunt them down. By this time 1 SAS had been joined by French SAS personnel and, in Algeria, Lieutenant-Colonel William Stirling, David's brother, had formed 2 SAS from 62 Commando. Later that month, David Stirling led a party west to provide a link between the Eighth and First Armies and contact his brother's SAS Regiment based at Bir Soltane. Choosing to risk the quicker route through the Gabes Gap, the party was intercepted by one of the German anti-SAS units and David Stirling was captured.

By end of the campaign in north Africa in May 1943, the SAS had lost both its leader and its specialised role. It survived by diversifying to

Below: A mass held in the Italian town of Cuneo, May 1945. Men of 2 SAS, who parachuted into the area to aid local partisans, are in the foreground.

Above: A Valetta aircraft drops supplies to a waiting SAS patrol in Malaya. Aerial supply was vital to teams operating for long periods in the jungle.

support Allied operations in the Mediterranean. Paddy Mayne took 250 officers and men of 1 SAS to Palestine to form the Special Raiding Squadron (SRS), which was meant to operate in the Balkans area but was ultimately used for commando/infantry duties in Italy. An equal number of men were formed into the Special Boat Squadron (SBS) to carry out amphibious raids on the enemy-held Dodecanese Islands. Meanwhile, 2 SAS continued to recruit and consolidate and was used to support the invasions of Sicily and Italy in 1943 as commandos

or deep-penetration raiders, striking at German lines of communication in northern Italy.

The Allied invasion of France in the summer of 1944 brought the various elements of the Special Air Service together. The SAS were joined by the two French Parachute Battalions (later 3 and 4 SAS), the Belgium Independent Parachute Squadron (later 5 SAS) and F Squad-

Above: Members of 22 SAS check their jump equipment before boarding Valettas, Malaya 1954.

ron GHQ Reconnaissance Regiment (Phantom), all under the overall command of the 1st Airborne Division. Some of the initial schemes employing the SAS in support of the invasion were unnecessarily dangerous, so much so that Bill Stirling resigned in protest. One example was the various 'Titanic' operations ('Titanic I-IV'), which dropped men into an area south of Carentan on the eve of D-Day. Their job was to fool the Germans into believing that an airborne division had landed, thereby diverting men and material away from the US landings farther to the north. With the SAS parties went dummy parachutists designed to explode on impact, thereby simulating rifle and machine-gun fire, and pintail bombs which released Very-light cartridges to give the impression of large-scale activity on the ground. Not surprisingly, the parties did nothing more than spend most of their time attempting to evade capture.

A French traitor opened fire with a submachine gun

As a consequence of pressure from the SAS themselves, the 41 subsequent operations in France and Belgium were more realistic. Most parties were dropped far behind the Normandy beachhead to disrupt communications and divert German troops away from the front. Operating in a 80km radius from their bases, the SAS sabotaged vital railways and used armoured jeeps to attack road convoys. The French *maquis* (resistance) proved to be enthusiastic, if inexperienced, fighters, but their security often left something to be desired and there were informers in their ranks. In the early hours of 5 July 1944, for example, a 12-man SAS party dropped into an area close to Paris. However, German troops and Gestapo already had the DZ surrounded and most were captured. When the prisoners were finally driven to a secret execution ground, the captives seized an opportunity to escape. However, only three made it back to Allied lines. At a reception in the 'Loyton' base area, a French traitor opened fire with a submachine gun as the SAS parachutists landed. The confused firefight which followed was only ended when the traitor was shot dead. ('Loyton' in fact was very successful. No less than two German divisions were diverted to curtail the 'Loyton' party's activities). Subsequently, although the SAS occasionally operated with the *maquis*, depending upon local circumstances, they preferred to conduct independent operations. For the most part, training and organising the partisans was left to other clandestine operators such as the inter-Allied 'Jedburgh' teams.

Other SAS parties also inflicted considerable damage on the Germans. The 153-man 'Houndsworth' force under Lieutenant-Colonel Mayne accounted for 70 vehicles destroyed, 220 enemy troops killed and 22 attacks on the railways which derailed six trains. 'Houndsworth' also supervised supply drops which armed 3000 *maquis* fighters. In his laid-back way, 'Paddy' Mayne jumped into France carrying a wind-up gramophone and his two favourite records: 'The Garden Where the Praties Grow' and 'Come Back Paddy Riley', and throughout the conflict Mayne toured his command in a civilian car dressed in full uniform.

On 1 September 1944, travelling towards the 'Kipling' base, Mayne and two other SAS men came across a *maquis* ambush. When the German convoy appeared, led by a 36mm 'quick-firer' (armoured car), the partisans disappeared, leaving the SAS to meet the convoy head on with a Bren and a single Vickers. After Lieutenant Goddard was killed spraying the 'quick-firer' at close range with gunfire, Mayne lost his temper and, gaining higher ground, poured machine-gun fire and lobbed grenades into the lines of Germans in the hedgerows.

Below: SAS conversing with the locals in Oman, 1959. Great emphasis is put on language skills.

Right: A Beverley drops supplies to men of D Squadron near the Jebel Akhdar, Oman, in 1959.

With great difficulty, Major Marsh persuaded Mayne to leave the battle site only to discover that their vehicle had disappeared. Undaunted, they took off cross-country and commandeered a civilian car before continuing their journey. For Paddy Mayne, this was 'just a little scrap'.

The involvement in France forged other legends. On 22 August 1944, Captain Derrick Harrison and elements of the 'Kipling' party drove their jeeps into the central square of Les Ormes where they interrupted an SS execution. Over 60 Germans were killed in the subsequent bloody engagement, allowing all but two of the condemned men to escape. Later that month, Roy Farren's 'Wallace' party attacked a chateau in the Chatillon area housing 150 enemy troops. German reinforcements fell into an SAS ambush and the raiders were credited with destroying nine trucks, four cars and a motorcycle. In addition, around 100 enemy personnel were killed.

Following the liberation of France, Roy Farren and 2 Squadron, 2 SAS, went to Italy where they directed partisan activity in the Tuscan Appenines. Ordered not to accompany his unit into action, Farren contrived to 'fall'

from the Dakota aircraft while despatching his men. Meanwhile, the rest of the SAS conducted jeep reconnaissance missions for the British and Canadian armies advancing into Germany. One of their last duties before being disbanded was to round up wanted Gestapo and SS officers. Even after the SAS had ceased to exist, a small number of ex-members semi-officially continued the search for Germans responsible for the torture and execution of SAS soldiers in France.

The often indiscriminate use of firepower occasionally hit 'friendlies'

It took an unusual war to resurrect the SAS. In 1948, a cadre of experienced guerrillas who had fought the Japanese in Malaya with Force 136 returned to the jungle to launch a Marxist-style war of liberation against the British. As a result, the disadvantaged rural Chinese squatter population which furnished the insurgents with supplies and recruits was moved into protected villages (*kampongs*). The guerrillas responded by growing their own food in their remote jungle bases and deepening links with the Aboriginal tribes in northern Malaya. Faced with mounting a military response to incidents where and when they occurred, one British officer decided that the security forces needed a unit that could take the war into the guerrilla sanctuary areas. That officer was 'Mad' Mike Calvert, an experienced special forces soldier who had served with the Chindits in Burma and commanded the SAS Brigade in Europe. His unit, the Malayan Scouts, drawn from local recruits, became A Squadron; 21 SAS, the British Territorial Army unit, formed B Squadron; and C Squadron was drawn from the Rhodesian Army. The British component of the force was enlarged and renamed 22 SAS Regiment in 1951. Four years later, the Rhodesians went home and were replaced by the New Zealand SAS Squadron.

Some of the SAS work in Malaya involved taking part in conventional operations such as Operation 'Hive' in the Negri Sembilan mountains, and Operations 'Termite' and 'Sword'. All these operations used both SAS and conventional infantry battalions and were designed to disrupt life in the guerrillas' own 'safe areas'. The problem with these large-scale operations

An SAS team rests while on patrol in Borneo. Four-man teams operated for weeks at a time to gather intelligence on Indonesian-backed insurgents.

was the often indiscriminate use of firepower, which occasionally hit 'friendlies' as well as the terrorists. The SAS decided that a better approach lay with the use of four-man long-range reconnaissance patrols, together with a determined 'hearts and minds' programme directed towards the indigenous population. Infiltrating guerrilla-controlled areas by parachuting into the jungle, patrols gradually built up a picture of enemy activity from well-used tracks, fields laid to rice, arms caches and camps. This information could then later be used to lay ambushes

and launch search and destroy operations. A number of terrorist leaders were followed back to their hide-outs and killed or captured by the SAS thanks to timely intelligence.

The SAS also developed the art of utilising the skills of indigenous personnel. Iban trackers from Borneo had much to teach the soldiers about scouting, while surrendered enemy personnel (SEPs) could lead the security forces back to arms caches and camps. The discovery of an arms cache allowed homing devices to be placed on equipment such as radio transmitters which, once collected, would lead the SAS to the guerrillas. An even more effective approach was winning over the Aboriginal tribes and persuading them to come into the forts that the

British built to dominate the jungle. Living inside the defended encampment, the Aboriginals were encouraged to form militias for their own protection, which further reduced support for the guerrillas. The Malayan campaign officially ended in 1959-60 when the remaining insurgents slipped across the northern border to create sanctuary areas in Thailand.

Malaya laid the blueprint for future SAS operations

Malaya laid the blueprint for future SAS operations, particularly those in Borneo. Indonesia, intent on dominating its nearby neighbours, clashed with Britain in Borneo. This time the insurgents who tried to foment rebellion were not guerrillas but regular soldiers, often Indonesian paratroops and marines. The parties of insurgents crossing the 1000km-long border of mountainous jungle were engaged upon sabotage missions or subverting the jungle tribes.

The SAS arrived in Borneo in January 1963 and was initially used to fill an intelligence gap. As many of the Indonesian parties were heading for the populated coastal strip, the security forces hoped to intercept them en route. Two- and four-man SAS surveillance posts were established across the length of the border to report on incursions. The surveillance network was greatly expanded by winning the hearts and minds of the jungle tribes and employing indigenous forces, for example the Border Scouts, in an intelligence gathering role. Reinforced and aided in no small measure by SAS contingents from New Zealand and Australia, 22 SAS embarked on the highly secret 'Claret' recce/strike operations to identify and attack enemy bases just inside Indonesian Borneo (Kalimantan). SAS activities made a significant contribution to victory in Borneo. The casualty rates alone were enough to persuade Indonesia that the incursions were not worth the effort involved. While essentially fighting a defensive war, Commonwealth forces killed more than 2000 Indonesians at a cost of 115 servicemen killed and around twice that number wounded — 22 SAS lost only three men killed and two wounded in nine operational tours.

A guerrilla base inside South Yemen was attacked and destroyed

At the beginning of the 1970s 22 SAS returned to Oman, where they had already achieved a legendary success in 1959 by storming the rebel-held Jebel Akhdar plateau in defence of the regime of the Imam of Oman, Ghalib bin Ali. Now, faced with the large-scale insurgency effort of the People's Front for the Liberation of the Occupied Arabian Gulf (PFLOAG) which was backed by neighbouring South Yemen, the monarchy was beginning to buckle, and there was a real threat to the flow of the West's oil through the Persian Gulf. The SAS, divided into individual British Army Training Teams

Above: The successful assault on the Iranian Embassy by 'Pagoda' Troop, 5 May 1980.

(BATTs), set about raising irregular militia (*firqat*) units from the locals and rehabilitated guerrillas.

By 1974, the Sultan's 15,000-strong force were augmented by 21 *firqat* units totalling around 1600 irregulars and administered by 50-100 SAS soldiers. Areas taken by conventional forces were subjected to an intensive hearts and minds programme by Civil Action Teams, which provided medical aid, wells, mosques, schools and markets. Once taken, these areas were never relinquished. In conventional military battles such as Mirbat, where a handful of SAS soldiers held off 250 guerrillas, and in the battles for the network of limestone caves on the South Yemeni border, the *adoo* — the guerrillas who fought against the Sultan's forces — lost heavily to the SAS and the Sultan's regular forces. When the guerrillas withdrew to form new bases they were pursued by *firqat* units, commanded by SAS or contract officers. Nowhere was safe for the guerrillas. In at least one instance, for example, a guerrilla base inside South Yemen was attacked and destroyed. The successful Omani campaign, which was as much about psychological warfare and civil action programmes as straightforward soldiering, cost the lives of only 12 SAS soldiers.

Between 1968 and 1974 the growth of international terrorism, coupled with a worsening situation in Northern Ireland, provided a new role for 22 SAS as a counter-terrorist force. A Counter Revolutionary Warfare Wing was set up at Hereford to provide instruction in the techniques of counter-terrorism, and Special Projects Teams received extensive training in hostage-rescue techniques.

The SAS deployment to Northern Ireland was first announced publicly in 1976, as the number of sectarian murders (247 in 1975) reached a crescendo in a series of particularly grotesque acts of terror. One area of the Province that received particular attention was South Armagh, known as 'Bandit Country', the heartland of the Provisional Irish Republican Army (PIRA.) The primary role of the SAS in

Northern Ireland was, and still is, intelligence gathering or reconnaissance, but the covert skills of the Regiment were ideal for 'sting' operations based on accurate intelligence about the movements of terrorists, 'safe houses' and arms caches. Two prominent members of the PIRA, Sean McKenna and Peter Cleary, were captured within the first few months of SAS operations. The Regiment quickly became feared and loathed by the PIRA.

The particular complexities and restraints governing operations in Northern Ireland were forcibly brought home in May 1976, when two parties of SAS where arrested by the Eire police after accidentally crossing the border. Neither did the SAS stock-in-trade surveillance operations always proceed smoothly. In July 1978, a serious breakdown in communications between the Army and the Royal Ulster Constabulary (RUC) resulted in an SAS surveillance team inadvertently killing John Boyle, an innocent 16-year-old schoolboy, when he returned to

Below: The Falklands, June 1982. Men of D Squadron prepare to be airlifted behind enemy lines.

Above: One of the SAS's most successful anti-terrorist operations in Ulster was the ambush at Loughall in 1987 in which eight terrorists died.

look at an arms cache that he had earlier accidentally discovered.

More ominously, SAS standard operating procedures (SOPs) were apparently not totally unknown to the PIRA leadership. According to Martin Dillon in his book *Dirty War*, a terrorist weapon implicated in several murders was bugged by the Security Forces and traced to a housing estate at the hamlet of Carness. On 19 February 1984, a two-man SAS surveillance team, commanded by Sergeant Paul Oram, mounted watch over the arms dump, supported by an SAS backup team in several cars. However, the 'tagged' weapon had been planted by a double agent already identified, interrogated and murdered by the PIRA. Possibly suspecting a 'sting', the terrorist leadership ordered the North Antrim Battalion to set up a two-man counter-surveillance post with orders to find and eliminate the SAS. On 21 February, Henry Hogan and Declan Martin spotted the SAS hide. Requesting orders, they were told to capture the soldiers that night. The SAS men were taken by surprise from the rear and, as they turned to fire, Oram was shot dead and his companion wounded. The two PIRA men then made a mistake which cost them their lives. By turning to escape without checking that both men were dead, they allowed the wounded soldier to send a radio signal to the SAS support team — both terrorists were subsequently intercepted and killed.

The black-clad counter-terrorist soldiers abseiled down the building

The SAS have always operated in hostile environments and Ulster has proved to be no exception. Against a background of missions that depend heavily on intelligence, enemy counter-intelligence and where a single mistake can prove fatal, the SAS have scored remarkable successes, not least the carefully planned operations that eliminated experienced PIRA murder squads at Loughall (May 1987), Omagh (August 1988) and Gibraltar (March 1988).

Although the PIRA took its campaign of terror on to the streets of Britain — a development monitored by the SAS — it was a different organisation that brought the Regiment international media attention. On Monday 5 May 1980, a Special Projects Team ended the siege at the Iranian Embassy staged by members of the self-styled Democratic Revolutionary Front for the Liberation of Arabistan. As the world watched, the black-clad counter-terrorist soldiers, amid smoke, explosions and gunfire, abseiled down the sides of the building and entered the Embassy to rescue the hostages. For many of those watching, it was the first time they had ever heard of an organisation called the Special Air Service. The Regiment has been trapped in the media spotlight ever since.

Troopers from D Squadron destroyed 11 enemy aircraft in a classic operation

The Falklands conflict which erupted in April 1982 gave the Regiment an opportunity to practise its specialist wartime roles of covert intelligence gathering and raiding. Throughout the campaign these tasks were shared with the Royal Marine's Special Boat Squadron. Reconnaissance teams, which spent many fraught days hidden behind Argentine lines locating, identifying and assessing the strength of enemy

forces, made a vital contribution to the success of the ground operations. However, the Regiment is more likely to be remembered for the more famous raid on Pebble Island on 15 May, when troopers from D Squadron destroyed 11 enemy aircraft in a classic night-time operation.

During the 1991 Gulf War, SAS teams were inserted inside Iraq and Kuwait to assist Allied conventional forces and to collect intelligence. Missions included locating strategic and tactical targets — communications headquarters, Scud surface-to-surface missile launchers and command bunkers — assisting Allied aircraft in destroying them by fixing them with hand-held laser designator devices. The beam would bounce off the target into the sky, creating a 'tunnel' down which a laser-guided bomb could travel. Other operations involved rescuing and evacuating downed Allied aircrew.

The SAS is currently part of UK Special Forces Group, which also includes the Royal Marines' Special Boat Service (formally Squadron). Two of the three SAS Regiments are part of the Territorial Army: 21 and 23 SAS. 22 SAS, the regular formation, is based at Stirling Lines in Hereford and consists of four 'Sabre' Squadrons (A, B, D, and G Squadrons) and an Army Reserve 'Sabre' Squadron (R Squadron). Each squadron is divided into four troops: Mountain, Boat, Mobility and Air Troop — each specialising in different modes of insertion or operational environments. Each troop consists of four four-man fighting patrols, each of which deploys a signaller, linguist, medic and demolitions specialist. All are cross-trained in one of the other patrol skills, for example the linguist may also be trained in demolitions, and all receive extensive training in long-range patrol techniques. The squadrons are supported by a Headquarters Squadron, Operational Planning and Intelligence (called the 'Kremlin'), Operational Research Wing, Counter Revolutionary Warfare Wing, Demolitions Wing, Training Wing and attachments from other Corps: signals (264 Signal Squadron), transport (Royal Corps of Transport) and a flight of the Army Air Corps ('S' Flight).

Left: As these two snipers illustrate, the SAS are experts in camouflage and concealment skills.

THE GREEN BERETS

Formed in the early 1950s, the US Green Berets are skilled in counter-insurgency and unconventional warfare. From the paddy fields of Southeast Asia to the jungles of Latin America, they have proved themselves to be masters of their art.

THE American Special Forces ('Green Berets') were formed to provide a reluctant US Army with an unconventional warfare capability, which it neither wanted nor understood. The nature of the special sort of war that the Green Berets intended to wage was embodied in their doctrines and included 'the organisation of resistance movements and operation of their component networks, conduct of guerrilla warfare, field intelligence gathering, espionage, sabotage, subversion and escape and evasion activities.' The Green Berets were thus very different from the World War II commando-type units and, while they adopted the traditions of the Rangers and joint US-Canadian 1st Special Service Force, their real parent was a more shadowy organisation called the Office of Strategic Services (OSS).

The American OSS had been formed to serve alongside the British Special Operations Executive (SOE) during World War II, raising guerrilla units and carrying out sabotage missions behind German and Japanese lines. The OSS

A Special Forces team in Kuwait City during Operation 'Desert Storm', February 1991. The 'dune buggy' Fast Attack Vehicle (FAV) was used operationally for the first time in the Gulf War.

Above: Special Forces in Vietnam. Teams from the 1st, 5th and 7th SFGA saw service in the conflict.

was also charged with gathering intelligence, so combining the two roles of the British SOE and MI6. At the end of the conflict the OSS was disbanded and its successor, the Central Intelligence Agency (CIA), was expected to confine itself to solely collecting information. The US Army wanted nothing to do with elites or with what they saw as spies, it wanted soldiers who fought from their own side of the lines.

The global situation map in the Pentagon appeared to be turning red

During the Korean War (1950-53), elite units were used without any centralised doctrine, strategy or command and control. A partisan force was raised to wage guerrilla warfare behind communist lines, but a singular possibility with even greater potential was missed. An indigenous anti-communist guerrilla movement, for example, was already operating in the rice belt of North Korea which, with a little more foresight by the Americans, might have become the focus of a carefully orchestrated rebellion. Attempting to fill this vacuum, Brigadier-General Robert McClure and three OSS veterans within the Special Operations Section (SOS) think-tank successfully lobbied the Pentagon for permission to create a small special warfare unit. On 20 June 1952, the 10th Special Forces Group (Airborne) — SFGA — was activated and tasked with operations in Europe, where it was thought the big East-West clash

would occur. It was based at Fort Bragg, North Carolina, a training base which was eventually to become the Special Warfare School.

During the 1950s and early 1960s, however, it became apparent that central Europe would not be the only area of conflict. From Indochina to Cuba, colonial or Western-orientated governments were overthrown by various revolutionary/nationalist movements, many of which looked to Moscow or Peking for support. To many US 'Cold War warriors', the global situation map in the Pentagon appeared to be slowly turning red. Teaching at the Special Warfare School became more specialised, concentrating on counter-revolutionary warfare doctrines, nation building and foreign internal defence, yet the US military still thought that these revolutionary forces could be fought by using the conventional tactics of search and destroy operations. However, as the US Army discovered in South Vietnam, hunting regular North Vietnamese Army (NVA) forces and Viet Cong (VC) guerrillas obscured the real nature of the conflict: the battle for the hearts and minds of the people. In 1961, for example, US intelligence estimates suggested that of the 35,000 VC fighting in the South, more than 34,000 had been recruited there.

The nascent Special Forces found a powerful ally in President John F. Kennedy, who

Above: A 107mm mortar at a remote CIDG camp in Vietnam opens fire during a Viet Cong attack.

believed that victory in Vietnam would require a 'whole new kind of strategy, a wholly different kind of force, and therefore a new and wholly different kind of military training.' The Special Forces were on hand to supply that new approach and they became part of Kennedy's vision of the 'brightest and the best' — Kennedy himself formally bestowed their first green berets. Special Forces teams were despatched to Vietnam to work with the CIA in what became known as the Civilian Irregular Defense Group (CIDG) programme. After Kennedy's visit to Fort Bragg in October 1961, four more groups were formed for deployment to Africa, the Middle East, Latin America and Southeast Asia.

The Green Berets were in fact already in Vietnam, having started to train units of the Army of the Republic of Vietnam (ARVN) in unconventional warfare. From 1957 the work of the 14th Special Forces Operational Detachment at the Nha Trang Commando Training Center had resulted in the formation of Vietnamese Rangers and the Special Forces, or Luc Luong Dac Biet (LLDB). The CIDG programme, however, was different. Training the Montagnard tribes in counter-guerrilla warfare was devised not only to wrest the Central Highlands of Vietnam from VC control, but also to provide a strategic buffer zone between Vietnam and the communist supply routes flowing down the Laotian and Cambodian borders. However, the fiercely independent hill tribes were outsiders in Vietnamese society. As they were also extremely poor, susceptible to disease, and only two tribes had any form of written language, nation building and motivation became the foundation of Special Forces programmes. The nature of this work was enshrined in the Civic Action Medal presented to the 5th Special Forces Group (SFG) in 1970,

which listed 49,902 economic aid projects, 10,959 medical projects and 34,334 education projects. In short, the 5th SFG had created 129 churches, 110 hospitals, 1003 classrooms, 398 dispensaries, 272 markets, 6436 wells, 1949km of road, 14,934 transportation depots and provided support for half a million refugees.

However, passive aid projects still left the strategic Central Highlands in the hands of the VC guerrillas, so the Special Forces set about training territorial militias to defend their own villages. Patrols were sent out into the countryside, exerting their influence in ever-wider circles — the counter-insurgency 'oil-spot' technique. Enemy-held villages were stormed and communist infiltration routes along the Cambodian and Laotian borders were watched and convoys ambushed. The programme was seeded by 10 'A-Teams' (each having 12 men), who worked with the Rhade tribe around Buon Enao in Darlac Province (1961-62). In 1963, the CIA handed over control of the programme

Below: A Special Forces reconnaissance team on patrol near the Laotian border, September 1966.

Above: Captain Roger Donlon in the CIDG camp at Nam Dong, 6 July 1964, following the VC attack.

to the Military Assistance Command, Vietnam (MACV). It continued to grow under the auspices of the 5th SFG, finally totalling 40,000 paramilitary soldiers and the same number of Regional Forces/Popular Forces personnel.

The camp was ablaze as phosphorus shells rained down on the compound

The VC and NVA fought back, placing Montagnard agents inside the camps to weaken them from within, before sweeping them away in human-wave assaults. On one occasion, 1000 VC guerrillas massed to assault the Special Forces camp at Nam Dong, a remote base close to the Laotian border in northern Thua Thien Province. The attack began at 0230 hours on 6 July 1964, and within hours the camp was ablaze as white phosphorus shells rained down on the compound. Two hours later, a gunship arrived ahead of reinforcements. Inside the camp, 55 soldiers lay dead with another 65 wounded, but Captain Roger Donlon, the Special Forces 'A-Team' commander (A-726), continued to organise resistance, despite being wounded in the stomach. His bravery and outstanding leadership won him the congressional Medal of Honor, the first awarded since the Korean War. The camp system continued after the Nam Dong incident, though with massive air and artillery support and the establishment of a special reaction force that could reinforce a besieged base at short notice.

The Mobile Strike Forces (Mike Forces) were the elite quick-reaction element of the CIDG camps. They also provided a reaction force for the CIDG long-range reconnaissance patrol (LRRP) teams within the so-called 'Greek-Letter Projects'. Operation 'Leaping Lena', for example, was initiated to teach the hill tribes the art of long-range reconnaissance patrolling: pinpointing enemy bases, supply dumps and infiltration routes for raids, ambushes and air strikes. This evolved into Project 'Delta', which employed reconnaissance and 'Road-Runner' Teams (CIDG personnel disguised as the enemy who hunted their foe deep in the jungle) inside the South Vietnamese border areas. Projects 'Sigma', 'Omega' and 'Gamma' quickly followed, employing a diverse range of ethnic minorities such as Cambodians, Chams and ethnic Chinese Nungs. The patrols were effective, but they needed a reaction force in order to capitalise on the intelligence gains and to get the LRRP teams out of trouble when they were discovered deep inside communist-controlled territory.

The Special Forces had not only discovered a way of taking the war to the VC, but also succeeded in turning the tactics of guerrilla warfare against the enemy. Buoyed up by their success, the reaction forces went over to the offensive and put their own reconnaissance teams into enemy territory to act as bait. When the communists ambushed the patrols, they themselves fell into a trap set by the Special Forces. The Mobile Guerrilla Force (MGF)

was created to mount long-term operations inside VC sanctuary areas. Each MGF usually consisted of an 'A-Team', one 150-man Mike Force and a 34-man combat reconnaissance platoon. Its task was to locate, observe and harass VC 'safe houses'. The Mike Force concept was so successful that it was expanded to support conventional forces. In 1967, all Mikes and MGFs were amalgamated into five Mobile Strike Forces, which were distributed throughout Vietnam under the control of Mobile Strike Force Commands (MSFCs). By the autumn of 1968, the five MSFCs were employing over

Above: A soldier of the 5th SFGA. The beret flash includes the colours of the South Vietnamese flag.

3500 Green Berets, who were supervising 7000 Mike Force personnel and 27,000 CIDG paramilitaries.

'Out of country' missions into Laos, Cambodia and North Vietnam all came under the control of the so-called Military Assistance Command, Vietnam/Studies and Observation Group (MACV/SOG). SOG itself was in turn controlled by the Special Assistant for Counterinsurgency and Special Activities (SACSA), answerable to the Joint Chiefs of Staff (JCS) in the Pentagon. Most of its personnel were drawn from the 1st, 5th and 7th SFGs, but it also included South Vietnamese Special Forces, CIDG personnel, Nung mercenaries and VC defectors. While the full range of 'black' propaganda and covert operations were conducted by various 'Study Groups', the largest being the Ground Studies Group (Oplan 34A and Ops 31). Forays into North Vietnam were coded 'Kit Cat', while 'Prairie Fire' and 'Daniel Boone' were targeted at Laos and Cambodia respectively. The immediate control of SOG operations was devolved to three Command and Control (CC) units covering the three cross-border combat zones: CC North (North Vietnam and Laos); CC Central (tri-border area) and CC South (Cambodia). Routine operations were launched from a number of fixed Command and Control Sites (CCS), leaving more covert operations to the Mobile Launch Teams. The primary operational units at each CCS were the Spike Recon Teams, composed of three Green Berets and nine indigenous soldiers.

While much of the work of SOG centred on cross-border intelligence operations to identify targets for strikes against supply lines and troop concentrations, it also ran a combat-rescue programme called 'Bright Light'. There were two types of 'Bright Light' mission. The first was designed to recover personnel who found themselves evading capture behind the lines ('evaders'). As these were usually pilots or long-range reconnaissance patrols, SOG worked in conjunction with the US Air Force Search and Rescue (SAR) organisation and local LRRP units. The overall success rate is still unknown, but the SAR calculated it could best assist those pilots who could be reached within 30 minutes. Nevertheless, some 'irrecoverable' personnel were rescued by the SEALs, Rangers or Spike Recons.

The second type of operation, aimed at recovering prisoners of war (POWs) and 'escapers', was less successful. Only one American serviceman was rescued but he later died of wounds; all of the 368 captives rescued in a series of successful missions were Vietnamese. It was against this background that a photo-graphic interpretation report sparked one of the most famous rescue operations, code-named 'Ivory Coast'/'King Pin'. A series of photographs taken at a place called Son Tay, 37km west of Hanoi, appeared to show a prison compound around which the prisoners' laundry had been arranged to spell out a SAR message: '55 POWs — six in need of urgent rescue.'

Simon's support group razed a barracks housing Soviet advisors

Politics and the labyrinthine structure of US intelligence both helped set back the rescue operation, and the detailed planning required for such a difficult and dangerous operation caused further delay. Other intelligence showed the presence of 12,000 NVA troops in the area: the 12th Infantry Regiment, based around Son Tay, in addition to a supply depot, artillery school and an anti-aircraft battery. The initial photographs were obtained in April 1970, but Brigadier-General Donald Blackburn, the Special Assistant for Counter-Insurgency and Special Activities, had to wait until 10 July before the mission received official sanction. The assignment went to Colonel 'Bull' Simons, who recruited a team of 50 Special Forces soldiers and 15 officers from personnel serving at Fort Bragg. The CIA built a mock-up of the prison at Eglin Air Force Base and the Defense Intelligence Agency (DIA) kept watch on orbiting Soviet spy satellites, so the complex could be dismantled just before they passed overhead. Despite the interruptions, the team was able to make 368 rehearsals, spending 1107 hours in the air.

The armada of HH-53 helicopter gunships and HC-130P tankers left the secret CIA base at Udorn, Thailand, at 2318 hours on 20 November 1970. The most up-to-date intelligence indicators were unfavourable, as both overhead reconnaissance and a North Vietnamese DIA agent suggested that the prisoners had been moved. Ahead of Simon's commandos, US aircraft saturated the radar and missile sites in the Hanoi area with ordnance. Four hours later, the helicopters were spraying the guard towers at Son Tay, while Simon's support group mistakenly razed a barracks housing Soviet advisors.

Major Dick Meadow's assault group landed in the prison yard only to find it deserted. The operation was not a total failure, however. The accuracy of the initial intelligence, together with the demonstration of the political will to mount a follow-up operation, allegedly shocked the North Vietnamese and led to an improvement in the treatment of American POWs.

The war in Vietnam cast a long shadow over US military thinking

The Special Forces effort in Vietnam was ended prematurely. Still out of favour with the military hierarchy, the 5th SFG left the country in December 1970, three years before the complete withdrawal of US conventional ground forces. The war in Vietnam cast a long shadow over US military thinking and the Special Forces withered in its shade. Seen as highly specialised, the 1st, 3rd, 6th and 8th SFGs were disbanded and the 5th, 7th and 10th Groups were reduced to a total of 3600 personnel. As a result, subsequent operations suffered greatly.

In 1961, the 7th SFG had begun conducting military assistance and advisory operations in Latin America, forming the nucleus of the 8th SFG which was based at Fort Gulick in the Panama Canal Zone. Fort Gulick housed the School of the Americas, which taught counter-insurgency methods to 44,000 Latin American soldiers. This teaching was followed up by Military Training Teams (Mil-Teams), who helped reorganise existing infantry battalions into Special Forces or Ranger units skilled in counter-guerrilla warfare. From 1955 to 1969, US aid helped establish Peruvian commando battalions, Chilean Special Forces and Airborne units, as well as Special Forces (Airborne) groups and elite infantry in the Dominican Republic, Venezuela, Bolivia and Colombia. Many of these countries also raised police commando units for urban counter-terrorist operations. However, in the post-Vietnam era America became more cautious. Aware that it had been American Military Assistance Teams that had begun the involvement in Vietnam, Congress prohibited Mil-Teams from entering combat zones and limited their stay within a country to six months only. Under the Foreign Affairs Committee of the House of Representatives, military assistance teams now took one of two

Left: Eagle Claw . Sea Stallions on the deck of the *Nimitz* before their flight into Iran. Mechanical problems with the aircraft doomed the operation.

Another component of the Mil-Teams was the elite counter-terrorist/hostage-rescue unit, Delta Force. The 1st Special Forces Operational Detachment Delta was formed in 1978, the brainchild of Colonel Charles Beckworth. Modelled loosely on the British SAS, the 400-strong force is divided into two operational and one support squadrons. While the parent unit specialises in counter-insurgency, Delta concentrates on counter-terrorism. Combined with SEAL Team Six, Delta is America's elite hostage-rescue unit. Personnel from the unit train the US Army in counter-revolutionary warfare at the Joint Readiness Training Center, Little Rock, Arkansas. Within the Mil-Teams, Delta instructors advise on counter-measures to defeat urban terrorist activities, such as hijacking and kidnapping.

Throughout the 1970s and 1980s, the United States found itself faced with revolutionary wars in its own 'backyard': Central America. The Nicaraguan civil war, for example, ended with victory for the Sandinista National Liberation Front (FSLN) over the dictator Somoza's troops on 19 July 1979. Soon after, the numerous opponents of the Sandinistas organised a counter-revolutionary force (Contras) in Costa Rica and Honduras, composed of former

forms: overt Military Training Teams — which visited 65 countries between 1983-84 — and more covert teams under 'deep' civilian cover. The majority of these personnel were Special Forces, SEALs or CIA covert operations staff.

Below: The ability to arrive undetected on a hostile shore is an essential skill for elite units.

members of Somoza's national guard — they were totally ineffective. However, in 1981 the Reagan Administration, alarmed that the Nicaraguans might export their revolution, especially to neighbouring El Salvador, ordered covert aid to the Contras. The CIA combined most of the groups into the Nicaraguan Democratic Force, provided training facilities in Guatemala and Florida and operational bases along the Honduran border. The Contras were given training by the Green Berets, CIA staffers, Cuban exiles and other soldiers of fortune recruited by the CIA. This 15,000-strong force was expected to wage a successful guerrilla war inside Nicaragua, but in fact was never involved in more than cross-border looting and commando raids. More recently, the Sandinistas held, and lost, national elections and President George Bush backed Honduran efforts to expel the Contras from their jungle bases.

The 5th SFG was involved in training personnel from the Saudi armed forces

One of the main reasons for supporting the Contras was the claim that the Sandinistas were arming the guerrillas in neighbouring El Salvador. In that country the US supported the government against six Maoist or Marxist guerrilla groups known as the Farabundo Marti National Liberation Front (FMLN). In December 1980, President Carter suspended military aid in response to widespread human rights abuses by the security forces and the guerrillas capitalised on the situation, launching a country-wide offensive in January 1981 that would have toppled the government had the new Reagan administration not resumed aid in July.

By 1986, the US was giving $133 million in military aid, including 55 Special Forces and 150 CIA advisors in the package. The conventional search and destroy tactics were discarded in favour of a mobile counter-insurgency war. Immediate Reaction Infantry Battalions, such as the elite Atlacatl Battalion, were used in helicopter-borne raids into guerrilla areas, while another six brigades of infantry were employed in the static defence of towns and key locations. Other units operated more covertly, such as the two Special Forces Groups, 1st 'Prial' (a long-

range patrol) and 2nd 'Hacha' (special operations). To combat this threat, the guerrillas moved into the villages and towns to wage an urban insurgency campaign. President Duarte began talks with the guerrillas in 1984 but was forced from office by ill-health. Meanwhile, the US Special Forces concentrated on civic action programmes to undermine the guerrillas' not inconsiderable support. At present, Roberto d'Aubuisson's right-wing ARENA party continues to confront an estimated 5000 experienced insurgents.

US Special Forces were also involved in the 1983 invasion of Grenada and the 1991 war in the Gulf. In Grenada, a unit from Delta was tasked with assaulting Richmond Hill Prison on the western side of the island and rescuing the prisoners, who would then be evacuated by helicopter. Unfortunately, the heliborne assault was delayed and by the time the Delta force reached the prison the Grenadans had fully alerted their anti-aircraft batteries. One UH-60 Black Hawk helicopter was shot down and the rest driven off by the hail of fire, bringing Delta's involvement in Operation 'Urgent Fury' to an ignominious end.

After Iraq had invaded Kuwait on 2 August 1990, US Special Forces were among the first units to be deployed to Saudi Arabia as part of Operation 'Desert Shield'. The three battalions of the 5th SFG, the 160th Special Operations Aviation Brigade and the Delta force began training for operations deep inside Iraqi territory. The 5th SFG was also involved in training personnel from the Saudi armed forces and the Kuwaiti resistance. The latter were taught how to ambush Iraqi units inside Kuwait, and to collect and pass on important intelligence.

Before the Allied land assault began on 24 February 1991, American Special Forces had infiltrated Iraq and Kuwait and were conducting a wide variety of missions. These included destroying Iraqi early warning radars before the air campaign began in mid-January, thus creating a 'corridor' through which Allied fighters and bombers could penetrate Iraqi air space undetected. In addition, Special Forces teams also saved downed Allied aircrew, reaching them before Iraqi forces and then guarding them until they could be evacuated by helicopter.

Other roles included sabotage, ambushes and intelligence gathering. The Special Forces fast attack vehicle was first used operationally in the Gulf War, and results have shown that it performed extremely well in the arduous desert conditions encountered in Iraq and Kuwait.

Above: A member of the 5th Special Forces Group in Kuwait City during Operation 'Desert Storm'.

The Special Warfare Center and School oversees all aspects of training

Today, the American Special Forces consists of the 10th Special Forces Group (operations in Europe and Africa), 5th (Southeast Asia & Pacific), 1st (Northeast Asia), 3rd (Sub-Saharan Africa), 7th (Caribbean, South & Central America), 11th (US Army Reserve, Fort Meade, Maryland), 12th (US Army Reserve, Arlington Heights, Illinois), 19th (Army National Guard, Salt Lake City, Utah) and 20th (Army National Guard, Birmingham, Alabama). On 1 October 1982, the Special Forces were reorganised into the 1st Special Operations Command (1st SOCOM (Airborne)) together with the 75th Ranger Regiment, Psychological Operations, a Special Operations Aviation Regiment, Civil Affairs Groups, signals and other support units. This then became the US Army Special Operations Command (USASOC) on 16 April 1987, joining the other services within the United States Special Operations Command (USSO-COM) — an umbrella organisation for all US special warfare units.

The John F. Kennedy Special Warfare Center and School (SWCS) oversees all aspects of Green Beret training. Staff at the School are responsible for the assessment and selection of personnel as well as running the Combat Diver, Military Freefall, Waterborne Infiltration and Target Interdiction courses that constitute advanced training. Other areas include PsyOps (motivating friendly forces and influencing enemy morale), Civil Affairs (which advises on indigenous peoples and their customs, and provides a vital link between field commanders and the local populace), Survival, Evasion, Resistance (to interrogation) and Escape (SERE), and Combating Terrorism.

The teaching branch also handles the promotion courses, such as the Operations and Intelligence Course required for master sergeant. The International Studies Department teaches foreign affairs and languages. The School taught a total of 8600 students in 1988 and expects to enrol over 14000 candidates annually a year by the early 1990s.

THE (A)SAS REGIMENT

The Australian SAS Regiment, like its British counterpart, is highly trained and superbly equipped. Formed during the Malayan Emergency, it saw extensive service in Vietnam, where it achieved a notably high kill rate. Since the late 1970s the Regiment has assumed a counter-terrorist capability, and is now rated by many experts as being among the best in the world.

TODAY'S Australian elite units have their roots in World War II. The Imperial Japanese Army came close to Australia's shores when it invaded New Guinea and the Pacific islands in early 1942. Across the Torres Straits the remote stations and small townships of sparsely populated northern Australia prepared to meet the enemy with guerrilla warfare.

Capitalising on their expert knowledge of the arid bush and deserts, the 2nd/1st North Australia Observer Unit was raised in July 1942 to conduct mounted patrols into remote, unmapped areas of the northern coast to report on enemy amphibious landings. In the event of an invasion, the 'Nackeroos' were to remain behind to report on the advancing Japanese forces. Across the sea, other groups, such as the civilian Coastwatchers and M Special Force, also collected vital intelligence from behind the lines, while the Australian Independent Commando Companies and Z Special Force took the war into the enemy's camp.

At the end of the war all but a few regular Australian Army infantry units were demobilised. The move towards a

The terrain of Western Australia is ideal for the realistic training necessary to keep the SAS in a high state of readiness. Here, two troopers are on a long-range patrol.

post-war elite airborne unit began on 23 October 1951 with the creation of an airborne platoon of the Royal Australia Regiment (RAR), which was tasked mainly with 'warfare tactical research', airborne search and rescue and providing assistance to civil authorities in national catastrophes. Based on Australian experiences in World War II, two Commando Companies were raised in 1955 but these were part of the reserve army or Citizen's Military Force. The subsequent formation of the 1st Special Air Service Company (Royal Australian Infantry) in April 1957 owed much to the success of the British SAS in Malaya and the need to contain the growing insurgencies in Southeast Asia. It was not an independent force but joined the Airborne Platoon as part of the RAR.

'Shoot and Scoot' frequently meant abandoning a wounded comrade

The primary role of the new SAS unit was medium-range reconnaissance: the insertion of parachutists deep into enemy territory to gather intelligence and other specified tasks until eventually relieved by conventional forces. The Company was organised on commando/infantry lines and was based at Swanbourne barracks, Perth. The men wore red berets with the crossed rifles of the Royal Australian Infantry Corps.

Requests for the usual specialist operational hardware — canoes, plastic explosives, commando knives, hand-cuffs and ropes — were treated with suspicion by the Director of Military Operations, who wanted to know why a medium-range reconnaissance unit would require such equipment.

The Company spent the next few years training in the hostile terrain of northwestern Australia. These exercises were not without incident, as Lieutenant-Colonel David Horner makes clear in his regimental history, *SAS: Phantoms of the Jungle*: 'Two other members of the company had to abandon a 12-foot rubber dingy when a crocodile climbed aboard. Sharks were in the area, but the two men gingerly pulled up the anchor and towed the dingy ashore with the crocodile as passenger.'

Deployment to Borneo in 1964, to join the British and New Zealand Special Air Service (NZSAS) fighting Indonesian insurgents, resulted in expansion and reorganisation. The SAS Company was disbanded and its links with the RAR severed in favour of an independent SAS Regiment (SASR) with two operational squadrons and a headquarters (HQ) Squadron

— a total of 15 officers and 86 other ranks. For a while the red berets were retained, however parachute-qualified personnel were entitled to wear the distinctive drooped SAS sabre squadron wings or 'moths'. The Australian regiment was also faced with developing new tactics for the 'low-intensity' wars in Southeast Asia. The nine-man platoons were dropped in favour of the British four-man patrols, and the Australians received the benefit of 22 SAS's hard-won experience of jungle warfare in Borneo.

However, the Australians soon showed themselves capable of innovation. One tactic that was not adopted was the British 'Shoot and Scoot' policy. In Borneo the patrol's 'Forward Scout' frequently bore the brunt of accidental contacts and firefights on the narrow jungle trails. 'Shoot and Scoot' often meant abandoning a wounded comrade who was left to find his own way back to the emergency rendezvous (RV). Instead, Australian SAS patrols laid down an intense barrage of suppressive fire, while using fire and movement to fall back on the rear man. Once the scout had passed the last man, the patrol withdrew until it was safe to form a defensive position, at which point the commander would decide to move to the emergency RV or, if the situation allowed, return to the point of contact to search for any missing men. The ability to improvise on patrol drills was to serve the Regiment well in Vietnam.

The British and Commonwealth SAS units had three major roles in the Borneo Confrontation. First, developing a comprehensive surveillance network among the jungle tribes with 'hearts and minds' patrols. Before medical and civil aid could be provided, contact had to be made with these remote, often nomadic peoples some of whom migrated back and forth across the border. These long patrols — one lasted 89 days — were dependent upon aerial re-supply and the goodwill of the tribesmen. Their second task was training and leading local indigenous units known as Border Scouts. The last role involved dangerous forays across the border — the so-called top secret 'Claret' operations — to identify staging posts used by

Right: The Australian SAS is one of the best trained counter-terrorist forces in the world.

the Indonesians for their incursions into Borneo. Once identified, enemy bases received the attentions of British mortar and artillery fire, while other SAS four-man patrols were sent out to ambush the rivers and tracks that supplied the enemy's jungle bases.

The Australian squadron was caught in a firefight

Occasionally, the SAS were asked to lead large forces of conventional infantry back across the border to hit concentrations of enemy troops. Despite the increased safety in numbers, these operations often proved to be more dangerous than the reconnaissance patrols. On 30 January 1966, a large squadron-sized force, composed of infantry and a depleted B Squadron from the British 22 SAS, supplemented by soldiers from the Australian and New Zealand Special Air Service units, was deployed to attack an Indonesian base on the Sekayan River, where it was

believed a large enemy force was assembling for a raid across the border.

The SAS squadron crossed the frontier unobserved, eventually reaching the river at dusk on 3 February. Intending to catch the Indonesians unawares at dawn the next day, the party crossed the river and, leaving a platoon of British infantry to cover the crossing, advanced along the river bank. Suddenly, the lead troop stumbled into the enemy camp and were immediately pinned down by small-arms fire. A small open shelter provided the only protection for three noncommissioned officers (NCOs) from the Australian 2 Squadron, who were caught in a firefight that the Indonesians were quickly winning with the help of a .30 calibre machine gun. To cover their withdrawal, one of the SAS soldiers threw a phosphorus grenade which, unluckily, struck an upright beam on the far side of the hut and bounced back to explode among the Australians themselves, setting a number of them alight, including one of their most experienced men, Sergeant John Coleman. Taking advantage of a slackening in the battle, Coleman and two other wounded men took cover in a water-filled ditch.

Suffering severe phosphorus burns and cut off from the rest of the squadron withdrawing across the river, the plight of the men became even more desperate when their operational commander, quite correctly, called in a heavy artillery strike on the camp. Still ablaze, and with the first shells exploding around them, the stragglers launched a frontal charge which cut right through the encircling enemy and another party of Indonesians on the trail of the retreating squadron. Once across the river, the long journey to the border RV became a nightmare for the badly injured soldiers, who were forced to crawl along pig trails, compasses in hand, to avoid any Indonesian survivors who might be looking for them. Reaching the border around dawn, the soldiers pressed on, finally reaching a Gurkha patrol camp around mid-morning.

The first SAS operations concentrated on intelligence gathering

The Australian soldiers' last operations in Borneo involved them in the hunt for several large parties of infiltrators. In August 1966, with the end of the 'Confrontation' in sight, the last squadron returned to its base in Perth. In fact, the Regiment had already been committed to another war and, several months earlier, a third SAS squadron (3 Squadron) had been deployed to Phuoc Tuy Province, Vietnam, as the 'eyes and ears of the 1st Australian Task Force'.

Below: The handling of small boats, such as the two-man canoe shown here, is one of the standard skills acquired by all members of the SAS.

From the Task Force base at Nui Dat, the first SAS operations concentrated on intelligence gathering and hitting small Viet Cong (VC) outposts.

Soon the VC struck back in force, culminating in the 6th Royal Australian Regiment's famous battle at the Long Tan rubber plantation on 18 August 1966, in which the VC 275th Division was badly mauled. In follow-up operations, four- or five-man SAS patrols searched for parties of VC who had survived the engagement. In these guerrilla-controlled areas,

Above: In Vietnam the SAS undertook LRRP work on behalf of the 1st Australian Task Force.

southeast of Saigon, contacts were frequent and soon the SAS had notched up such a high kill rate — in five years the Australian and NZSAS killed more than 500 enemy for the loss of one man killed by enemy fire and 27 wounded — that the army considered turning the Australian infantry over to the SAS patrol role. In captured documents the communists referred to the SAS as the *Ma Rung* or jungle ghosts and,

Above: Because Australia has no marine corps, SAS training stresses maritime activities.

like the World War II Z Force, the enemy put a price on their heads, reputedly $US5000 dead or alive.

The patrol that resulted in the single SAS death provides a fascinating picture of these operations and the advantages of operating with a five-man team rather than the traditional four-man patrol. On the 17 January 1967, an SAS patrol, commanded by Sergeant Norm Ferguson, was dropped by helicopter into an area of open grassland and secondary jungle northwest of Binh Ba, Phuoc Tuy Province, in the central plain of Vietnam. The tracks were often frequented by the guerrillas and sounds could be heard from a VC encampment nearby. The next morning, as the patrol began to circle the

enemy camp, an ambush was sprung from the patrol's left and Private Russell Copeman, the patrol's medic walking 'Tailend Charlie', was hit twice by enemy fire. In the middle of a firefight a four-man patrol can ill afford to lose firepower by carrying a wounded man, and Copeman expected to be left behind. However, as the patrol lay down heavy suppressive fire and moved through their ambush drills, Private John Matten, the radio operator, ran forward to Copeman's last position and engaged the enemy at close range. Then, covered by the white, drifting smoke from a phosphorus grenade,

Madden lifted the medic on to his shoulder and rejoined the rest of the patrol.

The patrol, hampered by the badly wounded man, managed to just keep ahead of the enemy search parties. Over the next hour, and with the enemy in almost continual contact, the patrol stopped only briefly to dress the medic's wounds and radio for a helicopter extraction. When the RAAF helicopter appeared overhead, Copeman and Matten were winched aboard but the enemy charged into the small clearing, despite a constant hail of fire from the helicopter door-gunner. The last man to be extracted was Sergeant Ferguson, who was forced to fire at a party of VC who rushed into the clearing while he was still dangling from the aircraft's winch rope. Private Matten's action in rescuing Copeman and dressing his wounds initially saved the medic's life. Massive internal bleeding was successfully treated at the field hospital but, sadly, Copeman died four months later from complications. Other SAS deaths included Corporal Ronald Harris, an Aboriginal, who was accidentally shot on patrol while returning from an observation post to the patrol lying-up position; one other accidental patrol shooting; a grenade accident; the loss of an SAS soldier during a helicopter extraction; and a death due to illness.

Below: On exercise in the 'bush'. Two SAS men help an injured comrade to a waiting helicopter.

During Australia's 10-year involvement in Vietnam, the SAS squadrons were usually rotated on nine-month attachments to the main Task Force. Long-range reconnaissance patrols (LRRPs) still formed the majority of the Regiment's work, but ambushes, raids and prisoner snatches were also undertaken. Some of the last operations included running LRRPs into dangerous VC sanctuary areas such as the May Taos Mountains. Other tasks included prisoner of war (POW) rescue operations ('Bright Light' missions) with the US SEALs, and providing a 'fire brigade' for conventional Task Force operations, which were so successful that the VC withdrew from Phuoc Tuy Province altogether. They only returned when the Australians departed Vietnam in December 1972.

TAG training included mock assaults on high-rise buildings

In the aftermath of the Vietnam War, the SAS were given two new roles inside Australia: conducting regional long-range surveillance patrols (LRSPs) in the vast northwestern deserts, and counter-terrorism. The final impetus to create an Australian hostage-rescue/counter-terrorist (HRU/CT) force was provided by the bombing of the Hilton Hotel in Sydney on 13 February 1978, allegedly carried out by the extremist Ananda Marga religious sect. A year later,

permission was given to establish the Tactical Assault Group (TAG) within SASR to provide specialist support for the Commonwealth Police. The Group was kitted out with tried and tested equipment from Britain's 22 SAS and was trained in close quarter battle and hostage-rescue techniques. While practising assaults on aircraft and other vehicles, TAG training also included mock assaults on high-rise buildings, emphasising portals of entry such as air-conditioning ducts and lift shafts.

Another unit, the Offshore Assault Team (OAT), drawn from the SASR and the Royal Australian Navy's Clearance Diving Teams, was made responsible for incidents involving the numerous oil and gas platforms in Bass Strait. Both organisations were later combined into a single Counter-Terrorist (CT) Force which consists of 1 SAS Squadron, 1 Signal Troop and the Commanding Officer's Command Group. Facilities for CT training are reputed to have cost $A22 million and include advanced electronic outdoor close quarter battle ranges, an outdoor snipers' range and numerous urban training scenarios at Swanbourne; a special urban CT complex and vertical snipers' range at Bindoon; and aircraft mock-ups at Gin Gin airfield, Western Australia. The CT Force provides routine security for VIPs and at important public events, for example the Commonwealth Games, and has been placed on Special CT Alert three times: after the bombing of the Israeli consulate in Sydney (December 1982); after a threat to blow up TAA aircraft (January 1983); and when the Australian Security and Intelligence Organisation (ASIO) reported the likelihood of Armenian terrorist attacks in Australia (August 1983).

Demolition Wing teaches all aspects of explosives and sabotage

The SASR currently consists of a Regimental Headquarters and six squadrons. 1 Squadron is part of the CT Force, while 2 and 3 Squadrons train for the Regiment's wartime role and are subdivided into a headquarters, freefall troop, water operations troop and a vehicle-mounted troop. Operationally, four- to six-man patrols are deployed depending on the task and man-ning levels. Radio communications are maintained by 152 Signals Squadron. A signals troop is attached to the headquarters of each 'Sabre' Squadron. Base Squadron is responsible for local administration and logistical support. It has the capacity to detach medical, mechanical, transport and catering specialists to the 'Sabre' Squadrons when they are deployed independently from the Regiment. Training Squadron is responsible for SASR selection and advanced training and is divided into six wings: Water Operations Wing conducts specialist courses for combat divers and small marine operations; Climbing/Survival Wing teaches basic survival skills and roping/abseiling techniques; Demolition Wing teaches all aspects of explosives and sabotage; Vehicle-Mounted Wing teaches navigation, maintenance and all other aspects of long-range vehicle patrols; and Reinforcement Wing conducts SAS selection and coordinates the reinforcement training cycle.

Specialist weapons are employed by units such as the CT Force

The SASR wears standard Australian Army uniforms with the distinctive sand coloured beret and the famous winged dagger SAS badge. British Special Air Service-type straight-topped parachute wings are usually worn on the right upper sleeve. Weapons used by the Regiment include the Browning High Power handgun, the L1A1 SLR and the M16 rifle. In addition, the compact 5.56mm Steyr AUG assault rifle, issued to the Australian Army, is also available for field use. The M60 machine gun and M68 fragmentation grenades are also available when required. Specialist small arms, such as the Heckler & Koch series of submachine guns, the Israeli Galil rifle and the Parker Hale Model 82 sniper rifle, are employed by specialised sub-units such as the CT Force. Overall policy, planning, liaison and coordination of SAS operations is handled by the Director of Special Action Forces at the Army Office in Canberra.

Right: An Australian SAS trooper, weighed down with M60 ammunition, on active service against the Viet Cong, 1968. First deployed in 1965, the Regiment left Vietnam six years later.

FIGHTING TERRORISM

Faced with the threat of hostage-taking and general terrorist attacks against their peoples, Western governments have established crack counter-terrorist units. Each one is maintained in a high state of readiness to combat the menace.

S INCE the 1970s the rise in international terrorism has resulted in the creation of highly trained, dedicated counter-terrorist/hostage-rescue units (HRUs). This has been achieved with an eye to efficiency, cost-effectiveness and politics. The American Special Forces decided to create an independent counter-terrorist unit known as Delta Force, whereas the British Special Air Service (SAS) chose to rotate all of its 'Sabre' Squadrons through counter-terrorist training and duties. Other European countries, notably France, Belgium and Germany, have adopted the alternative model of creating counter-terrorist units from national paramilitary police forces.

Germany's famous *Grenzschutzgruppe* 9 (GSG 9) — Border Marksman Group 9 — was formed in response to Germany's humiliation following the murder of 11 Israeli athletes at the 1972 Munich Olympic Games. As an independent unit within the Federal German Border Police, or *Bundesgrenzschutz*, GSG 9 has both powers of arrest and national authority. Like other counter-terrorist units, the Germans are highly skilled marksmen who are trained to rescue hostages from every potential siege situation. They are also highly educated police officers who are not only trained in close personal protection, but also specialise in

Two members of Spain's crack counter-terrorist force, GEO. The unit has a strength of 120 men and is divided into 24 five-man teams. The man on the left is holding an MP5SD.

intelligence and advanced police work, spearheading their country's drive against terrorism.

Based at the Federal Border Guard base at Hangeler on the northern outskirts of Bonn, GSG 9 has an operational strength of around 200 men divided between a headquarters unit, five 30-man combat teams (Strike Units), a communications unit, an engineer unit, a training unit, a flight of helicopters and logistic backup. The Strike Units themselves each consist of a command element and five combat teams, called *specialein-satztrupp*, which provide the basic operational modules. Each combat team has a team commander, grenadier, coverman, pointman and marksman. In a hostage situation, the marksman and coverman provide support fire for the assault team of grenadier and pointman. The team commander is also expected to coordinate the assault and pass on any instructions from the unit commander.

In common with other elite military units, the combat team members are expected to rotate through all the combat team specialisations so that the small unit will not be crippled if one or more of the team is killed or wounded during an operation. At any one time there is a Strike Unit on stand-by to deal with any major terrorist incident within Germany or overseas.

Strike Team Three is highly trained in HALO parachute techniques

Further specialisation at Strike Unit level reflects GSG 9's close relationship with the British SAS. Strike Team Two, for example, is composed of combat swimmers. These men, who specialise in maritime operations, pay particular attention to the German oil rigs in the North Sea and the Baltic — they also provide worldwide cover for their country's large tanker fleet. Strike Team Three is highly trained in high-altitude, low-opening (HALO) parachute techniques, which they employ as a means of silently infiltrating a terrorist-held area. The other Strike Teams, trained in surveillance and close personal protection duties, operate in support of the police anti-terrorist division and the individual state counter-terrorist units. GSG 9 officers wear the standard green uniforms of the Border Guard, with the two

distinguishing features of *fallschirmjaeger* parachute wings and a dark green beret that bears the unit cap badge — a gold Prussian eagle flanked by oak leaves cluster.

GSG 9 was allowed to attempt a rescue at dusk on 17 October

Many elite units that have survived the passage of time have, at one time or another, been led by an outstanding personality and GSG 9 is no exception. Its first commander was the charismatic Ulrich Wegener, a 15-year veteran of the Border Police and an expert on counter-terrorism. Wegener is said to have accompanied the Israeli commandos on their Entebbe rescue in July 1976, but his greatest success was the storming of the hijacked Lufthansa 737 at Mogadishu, Somalia, in October 1977. Flight LH181, 'Charlie Echo', was seized by the notorious Baader-Meinhof Group — the Red Army Faction (RAF) — while en route from Majorca to Frankfurt, and finally flown to Mogadishu airport. Faced with the terrorists' threat to blow up the aircraft and its passengers, GSG 9 was allowed to attempt a rescue at dusk on 17 October (Operation 'Magic Fire'). The ensuing forced entry and brief firefight that left all but one terrorist dead and successfully rescued all the hostages rightly earned GSG 9 international fame.

From the outset of his career, Ulrich Wegener realised that terrorism could only be defeated by close international cooperation, with free exchange of intelligence, training and technology. Consequently, GSG 9 has played a major role in this area. Wegener himself was consulted prior to the SAS assault on the Iranian Embassy (5 May 1980), and took two SAS advisors and their stun grenades to Mogadishu. During the planning phase of Operation 'Eagle Claw' in April 1980 — the abortive attempt by Delta Force to rescue 53 Americans held hostage in Tehran by Iranian revolutionaries — Wegener offered to infiltrate a team of GSG 9 operators into Tehran to obtain the intelligence

Right: A GIGN team practises roadblock skills. Constant training to maintain a high state of readiness is essential for counter-terrorist units.

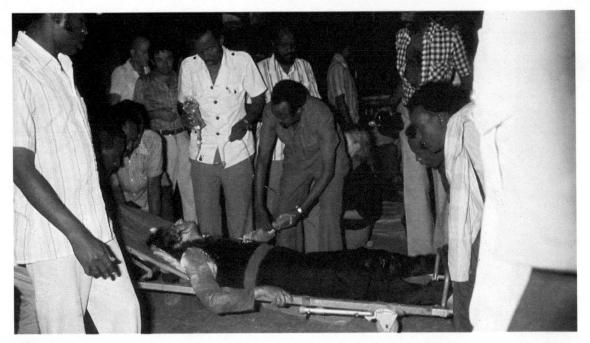

needed to rescue the US hostages. For reasons still not clear, his offer was refused. GSG 9 officers were present at the scene of the South Moluccan train hijack at Assen, Holland, in May 1977 to advise the Royal Dutch Marines as they prepared to launch the rescue operation. GSG 9 even provided training for six Georgia state troopers prior to the 1988 Democratic convention in Atlanta, and was the only unit prepared to train the Egyptian Force 777, following the latter's disastrous rescue attempt in Malta (September 1978) which resulted in the deaths of 57 passengers.

Dee inserted a five-man team and set up surveillance from a hide

GSG 9 also hosts the prestigious annual international combat team competition for special units, known as the 'Counter-Terrorist Olympics' unofficially. Each of the 22 participating countries enters two teams which are usually drawn from different national units. The events that take place over about a week include combat shooting and realistic rescue scenarios, as well as timed endurance events that involve an assault course and abseiling. Some idea of the units attending this exercise can be gleaned from the results of the 1985 competition, in

Above: Suhaila Sayeh, the only terrorist to survive GSG 9's assault on the Boeing 737 at Mogadishu.

which the South Bavarian Police were overall winners, followed by Delta Force, with the US Navy SEALs taking third place.

Following Wegener's promotion to deputy commander of the German Border Guard, leadership of the unit was given to Lieutenant-Colonel Uwe Dee. While it might be thought that Wegener would be a 'hard act to follow', 'Easy Dee's' domestic operations were as damaging to the RAF terrorists as Operation 'Magic Fire'. In October 1982, it was reported to the police that there had been unusual activity in a wood on the outskirts of Frankfurt. Dee inserted a five-man team and set up surveillance from a hide overlooking freshly dug ground. In a heavy snowfall the surveillance team waited patiently for five days, then, on the sixth day, two people appeared, crawling through the undergrowth to their hide. The captives were two top female terrorists and, much more importantly, the cache contained weapons and explosives, various forged military passes, registration papers for stolen cars, reports on American bases and the movements of German politicians. It also contained maps showing the locations of 14 other supply dumps and hides.

All were placed under surveillance and, only five days later, Christian Klar, one of the most important figures in the RAF, was captured at another supply dump near Hamburg. The state prosecutor, Kurt Rebmann, described the arrests as a 'catastrophic blow' to the RAF.

The strike units rotate onto active duties one week in four

In November 1973, the French Government formed its national counter-terrorist unit from the 'oldest serving regiment in the French Army': the *Gendarmerie Nationale* — a 60,000-strong paramilitary police force under the overall control of the Ministry of Defence. Tasked with handling politically sensitive hostage sieges, prison riots and the transport of dangerous criminals, the counter-terrorist unit is designated the *Groupement d'Intervention de la Gendarmerie Nationale* (GIGN).

From the outset GIGN was moulded by an extraordinary man, Lieutenant Christian Prouteau, who quickly stamped his personality on the men under his command. A black belt in karate and a keen athlete, Prouteau greatly influenced the unit's training — all recruits were expected to qualify as both parachutists and combat swimmers, as well as take a keen interest in mountain sports and 'hard style' karate. Originally, the unit was split into two sub-commands, with GIGN-1 covering operations in northern France from a base in the Parisian suburbs at Maisons-Alfort, and GIGN-2 responsible for operations in southern France and based at Mont-de-Marsan. In 1976, GIGN was streamlined into a unified command based in Paris.

As the French administration grew to appreciate the value of a low-profile police counter-terrorist unit, GIGN was given additional responsibilities and, as a consequence, increased manpower. By the late 1970s the unit had 40 noncommissioned officers (NCOs) and two officers, all organised into three basic strike units. The individual strike units each consisted of two five-man intervention teams, a team commander and a dog handler. In 1982, President Mitterand gave Prouteau a formal charter of 'coordination, investigation and action

against terrorism', and the unit was enlarged to provide security for sensitive installations such as nuclear power stations. A year later, GIGN was given the additional responsibility of providing a team to protect the President of the Republic. GIGN was permitted to establish an additional strike unit of 12 NCOs and, with each strike unit now commanded by an officer, the total unit strength increased to 54 policemen.

One of the strike units is always on 24-hour stand-by and is prepared to deploy to anywhere in the world at 30 minutes notice. The strike units rotate onto active duties one week in four. When an intervention team is called out, it is usually commanded by the senior NCO on the team or the officer commanding the strike unit, depending on the sensitivity of the mission. GIGN members wear a black uniform, complete with the unit flash (a parachute canopy over a wave-tossed sea) on the left shoulder and the famous French metal parachute wings on the right breast.

Both sieges were terminated with precision sniper fire

It was Prouteau's insistence on such high standards that led to the unit's great successes: at Djibouti in February 1976, when the unit rescued French school children held on a hijacked bus by members of the Front for Liberation of the Coast of Somalia; and at Clairvaux prison in January 1978, when two violent inmates seized a deputy warden and two prison officers. Both sieges were terminated with precision sniper fire. Like other crack counter-terrorist teams, GIGN has 'hardened' the security of French embassies in high-risk countries such as the Lebanon and El Salvador. In total, the unit has rescued over 250 hostages since its creation.

Holland has raised its counter-terrorist unit from the elite Royal Netherlands Marine Corps (RNLMC). The 2800-strong force is divided into three operational commands: Home Command (based at Rotterdam), Antilles Command and Corps Command. The latter is responsible for training and operations, while the other two Commands each deploy an amphibious combat group (ACG). The 1st ACG specialises in arctic warfare and, in the event of a general European war, it would join British, Canadian and American amphibious units in the defence of NATO's vulnerable northern flank. The Group spends three months every year in Norway, taking part in the annual winter warfare exercises. While in Norway, the Dutch Marines come under the overall control of Britain's 3 Commando Brigade. The 2nd ACG has a similar structure to its counterpart, with 700 Marines divided into three rifle companies. Based in the Dutch Antilles, 2nd ACG specialises in jungle warfare and takes part in the annual amphibious exercises held in the Caribbean. In addition to its NATO role, the RNLMC also has a United Nations commitment and maintains units on 24-hour stand-by for peacekeeping duties.

One independent unit within the RNLMC, 'Whiskey Company', is an integral part of 3 Commando Brigade for five months of the year. Most of its members are parachute trained and many have qualified as combat swimmers with the Dutch Special Boat Section (7 (NL) SBS), or as Mountain Leaders with the British Royal Marines' Mountain & Arctic Warfare Cadre. 'Whiskey Company' has two main roles: to train the ACGs, 7 (NL) SBS and the Company Boat Group in winter warfare techniques; and to provide personnel for the Dutch national HRU or Marine Close Combat Unit.

The Marine Close Combat Unit is divided into a HQ unit and three 33-man platoons. One platoon is always on 24-hour alert supported by a second platoon on stand-by. The third platoon acts as a training cadre, providing a 16-week initial training programme for recruits to the unit. Further training is provided by GSG 9, the British SAS and the Royal Marines' Comacchio Company. Additionally, the Combat Unit conducts realistic exercises at Schiphol Airport and Holland's many ports. The Marines' hostage-rescue unit was first employed at Schevengingen Prison in October 1974 to end an incident involving a jailed Palestinian terrorist. In the early hours of the morning, the lock on the prisoner's cell door was cut with a thermal lance and stun grenades

Right: Two members of GIGN equipped with night vision goggles and H&K submachine guns.

Above: Food is taken to the train seized by Moluccan terrorists in May 1977.

thrown in as a distraction, allowing the prisoner to be subdued without the intervention of lethal force. Training emphasises the use of non-lethal force, which is appropriate to the unit's extended brief of intervening in civilian riots.

However, the Marines are always prepared for situations that require more aggressive measures. Roughly half are trained snipers and three marksmen are always assigned to each target to eliminate as many terrorists as possible before the five-man teams attempt a rescue. The unit was first put on alert when South Moluccan terrorists hijacked a Dutch train in December 1975, but the siege ended without the need for armed intervention. In May 1977, however, nine South Moluccan terrorists simultaneously seized the Bovensmilde elementary school and a passenger train on the main line between Groningen and Assen. At the school, 110 children were held by four terrorists under conditions that quickly resulted in the outbreak of disease. Subsequently, the terrorists released all but four of the children. Meanwhile, on the train, a further nine terrorists held 51 civilians captive. Marine combat swimmers approached the train using a nearby canal and placed a variety of sensitive surveillance devices on the carriages. Similar devices were also placed around the school.

After three weeks of talks, a psychiatrist, negotiating on behalf of the police, decided that the situation had become very dangerous for the hostages and the Combat Unit was given permission to implement a rescue. Under cover of darkness a force of 50 Marines, divided into multiple five-man assault teams, simultaneously approached the train at a number of points. Above, six F-104 Starfighter aircraft flew low over the train to provide a distraction, while snipers began to fire into the carriages at terrorist sleeping areas, which had been pin-pointed by the surveillance equipment. After blowing the carriage doors with frame charges, the Marines took control of the train, killing six terrorists and capturing the other three. Two hostages were killed when they panicked and moved into the line of fire. Simultaneously, in a second operation at the school, all of the terrorists were captured alive, though somewhat dazed, and the four children released when assault teams in an armoured personnel carrier drove straight through the wall of the room in which the terrorists were sleeping.

Almost every country in the world has been touched by terrorism

The Combat Unit was used again, in March 1978, when South Moluccan terrorists seized a government building in Assen. The building was finally stormed when the terrorists carried out their threat to kill a hostage. The remaining hostages were successfully released, although six were wounded in the crossfire.

Almost every country in the world has been touched by terrorism, against which neither geographical location nor political neutrality serves as a defence. Even New Zealand, in its own remote corner of the world, has experienced two terrorist bombings; the first at the Trades Hall in Wellington and, second, the sinking of the Greenpeace ship *Rainbow Warrior* by French intelligence agents. Each resulted in the death of one person. In developing a response to potential terrorist incidents, the New Zealand Government has placed emphasis on timely, very reliable intelligence

Left: A Moluccan terrorist in Amsterdam, 1975. Despite being a small, peaceable nation, Holland has had to establish an effective anti-terrorist unit.

Left: Many terrorists are well armed and equipped. A PLO fighter with an RPG-7 rocket launcher.

enabled the communists to continue fighting in these last sanctuary areas.

Disbanded after their tour in Malaya, the Squadron became part of the permanent New Zealand order of battle in 1960. Two years later, the Squadron was deployed to Thailand to support US counter-insurgency efforts to combat the threat from communist guerrillas. The following year the NZSAS were renamed 1st Ranger Squadron to commemorate the 100th anniversary of the Forest and Taranaki Rangers — two early units which had fought in the Maori Wars in the nineteenth century.

The unit released all the hostages from a hijacked Boeing 737 at Luxor Airport

Over the next few years the Squadron was involved in two more jungle conflicts. Between 1965 and 1966, four detachments served with the British and Australian SAS during the Borneo 'Confrontation', where they faced various incursions by units of the Indonesian Army. In November 1968, a party made up of 25 men and an officer (designated 4 Troop) was sent to Vietnam to form an important part of New Zealand's contribution to the war effort. Based at Nui Dat in Phuoc Tuy Province, the Troop operated under Australian SAS command and, like the Australians, conducted reconnaissance and ambush operations ('recce-ambush') against Viet Cong (VC) and North Vietnamese Army (NVA) units. Occasionally, the Troop also operated with the American Special Forces, US Navy SEALs and the Marine Recon along the northern borders of Phuoc Tuy Province. Farther afield, the NZSAS are reputed to have trained Khmer Serei mercenaries and provided instructors for the Civilian Irregular Defense Group (CIDG) Program.

Today, 1 NZSAS Squadron is still small, consisting of five 12-man troops, a headquarters and a small training cadre. Additionally, there is a small nucleus of Territorials who undergo the same training and selection as the regulars. As a consequently, the counter-terrorist role is treated in exactly the same manner as

supplied by the police and the Security Intelligence Service (SIS), harnessed to a rapid response by the hostage-rescue unit deployed by the No 1 New Zealand SAS Squadron.

The NZSAS was formed in 1955, when New Zealand offered to send troops to Malaya in accordance with the ANZAM treaty, and was asked to provide a replacement for the Rhodesian SAS Squadron. The New Zealanders subsequently spent two years in Malaya and were credited with the deaths of 26 communist terrorists, including three area leaders. More importantly, the NZSAS made a vital contribution to the 'hearts and minds' programme. One third of the NZSAS soldiers were Maoris, who proved most able in building a rapport with the Aboriginal tribes of Northern Malaya. With great patience the tribes were coaxed into jungle forts and organised into armed militias for their own defence. The programme successfully severed the supply of food and recruits that had

Above: Scenes of joy as the civilians rescued at Entebbe arrive at Lod airport on 4 July 1977.

their other commitments. Probably for the same reason, they are said to favour well-tested soldiering skills over hi-tech counter-terrorist equipment. During a demonstration of counter-terrorist skills staged for a New Zealand Prime Minister, the politician and his entourage were left in a room with a terrorist dummy. In a display of live-firing, the SAS soldiers blasted open the door and eliminated the 'terrorist' in seconds. The politicians were reported to have been left 'amazed, dazed and deafened'.

The counter-terrorist units of some other countries have discovered the dangers of treating this military speciality too lightly. Egypt's premier anti-terrorist unit, for example, was formed from a para-commando unit that had seen extensive fighting in Yemen and in the wars against Israel in the 1960s and 1970s. Codenamed *Saiqa* (Thunderbolt), the unit successfully released all the civilian hostages from a hijacked Boeing 737 airliner at Luxor Airport in southern Egypt in 1975. However, disaster overtook the Egyptian HRU three years later when, in March 1978, two Palestine Liberation Organisation (PLO) assassins shot dead a close friend of Egyptian President Anwar Sadat in Nicosia, Cyprus. The terrorists, with 15 hostages in tow, were given safe conduct and a Cypriot DC-8 airliner to take them to a friendly Arab country. However, as all countries closed their airports to the plane, it finally had to return to Cyprus, where the authorities successfully negotiated the release of the hostages. However, a 54-man team from *Saiqa* arrived unannounced in Nicosia under the guise of 'negotiators' and, presumably thinking that the terrorists were about to evade justice once again, began to storm the aircraft. The resulting firefight with the Cypriot National Guard left 15 Egyptian commandos dead and *Saiqa*'s reputation in tatters.

A new Egyptian counter-terrorist unit was formed in 1978 from the Army Commando Command and designated Force 777. It also mismanaged an overseas operation, when Egypt Air Flight 648 was hijacked by terrorists and flown to Malta in September 1985. After the terrorists had murdered five passengers, the

Below: Dead passengers, shot by Egyptian snipers in error, lie on the airport tarmac in Malta.

Maltese Government reluctantly gave permission for an Egyptian assault. The subsequent operation, however, suffered from a dire lack of intelligence and overall planning.

No stun grenades were used, the Egyptians went in 'cold'

When the assault teams forced their way into the aircraft the terrorists were waiting (they had heard the cargo bay door being opened by the assault group). In addition, no stun grenades were used, the Egyptians went in 'cold'. To make matters worse, when the Egyptians detonated a charge in the cargo hold to act as a distraction, it only served to fill the cabin with smoke. As a result, many passengers were killed by smoke inhalation. More died as they fled the aircraft, shot down by Egyptian sharpshooters in the mistaken belief that they were escaping terrorists. Of the 98 passengers aboard Flight 648, no less than 57 were killed in the assault to free them. One obvious lesson to be learnt from the two Egyptian operations is that all counter-terrorist operations require planning skills way beyond the usual elite unit military training.

WEAPONS AND EQUIPMENT

To carry out their high-risk missions, elite forces require a wide range of military hardware but, of all the different pieces of equipment used by today's special forces, the personal weapon is still the most important.

ELITE forces throughout the world employ a wide variety of weapons and military equipment, ranging from handguns, submachine guns (SMGs) and automatic rifles to air-portable vehicles, specialised aircraft and high-speed assault craft. To cover this wide subject in any detail would require a large volume in itself, therefore only a summary of the more popular kit used is possible.

Special forces units undertake a wide range of operations which are notably different to those of conventional infantry forces. The latter are trained to operate on the battlefield as components of a large military machine and are supported by armour, artillery, helicopters and aircraft. Special forces, by comparison, often fight as small-sized, unsupported teams deep behind enemy lines. Each team member must be highly proficient in the use of his individual weapon, but the weapons themselves, to serve him in his mission, must also fulfil certain criteria, which are:

1) Absolute reliability. As special forces missions often involve short, violent contacts with the enemy, a reliable weapon is essential. They must work first time, every time.

The SA-80 is the new individual weapon of the British Army. Lightweight, well-balanced, easy to strip and clean, it is an ideal rifle for units such as the Parachute Regiment or SAS.

Rifles such as the Soviet AK-47 are crude by Western standards, but a *spetsnaz* team using them knows that they can always be relied upon, even when caked in mud or covered in snow. Similarly, SAS hostage-rescue units (HRUs) know that their MP5 series submachine guns (SMGs) will always work first time during a siege-busting operation.

2) Weight. As many special forces missions are conducted on foot and over difficult terrain, it is essential that individual weapons be as light as possible, and weight is of even more importance to elite airborne troops who are required to manhandle their equipment into combat. Paradoxically, over the last 60 years the trend has been towards heavier assault rifles — a consequence of the increasing complexity of internal working parts. The .303 Lee Enfield weighed 4.10kg loaded, compared to 4.30kg for the 7.62mm L1A1 Self-Loading Rifle (SLR), 3.6kg for the Soviet 5.45mm AK-74 and 4.98kg for the new British 5.56mm L85A1 (SA-80). The increased use of plastics in the construction of weapons, especially in the Heckler & Koch G11, the SA-80 and the innovative Glock range of handguns, seems set to reverse this trend. Though the overall weight of the infantry rifle has increased since World War II, the change to smaller calibre ammunition means that individual rounds weigh less than their predecessors, enabling more to be carried by individual soldiers.

3) Size. The length of a weapon determines its manoeuvrability and the ease with which it can be fired from the range of positions — sitting, prone, shoulder or hip — essential for special forces work. With the exception of the L1A1, later rifles have been shorter than the old Lee Enfield: Lee Enfield (113cm), L1A1 (114cm), M16A2 (94cm) and SA-80 (78.5cm). The MP5K series used by SAS and other HRUs is only 32.5cm long.

4) Maximum firepower. The 1980s witnessed the introduction into service of a number of weapons which had smaller calibres than their predecessors, such as the SA-80 which replaced the SLR and the AK-74 which replaced the AK-47. The smaller 5.56mm cartridge resulted in an overall reduction in weapon size and recoil. In addition, the round displayed an increased lethality when compared to the older and heavier 7.62mm bullet, as it 'tumbled' rapidly when it hit the target and delivered its energy in a massive fashion rather than passing through the target with minimal energy transfer. This latter problem is especially true of the standard 9mm round, which has a tendency to pass straight through the body of a victim and keep on going. FBI files, for example, contain documented cases where felons were hit with 30-40 9mm bullets during the course of long firefights and still continued to fight, and even kill several officers, before themselves receiving a mortal wound!

The weapon is sealed to prevent the intrusion of water and dirt

Looking towards a combat rifle for the twenty-first century, the American Army's Advanced Combat Rifle (ACR) Program is considering four prototype rifles which may be used to design a Future Individual Combat Weapon to replace the current M16A2. Conducted jointly by Army Armament Research, Development and Engineering Center (ARDEC), Army Training and Doctrine Command (TRADOC) and Joint Services Small Arms Program (JSSAP), the ACR Program is designed to test the candidate weapons under conditions of simulated combat stress. This was deemed important as, while the M16A2 is capable of producing 100 per cent hits at 300m and an 80 per cent score at 600m, these figures have been shown to drop dramatically in a 'combat environment': 20 per cent at 100m, 10 per cent at 300m and only five per cent at 600m. Consequently, the prototype weapons are being examined for their capability to increase the probability of hitting the target under battlefield conditions. This has led some observers to speculate that the US Army is trading-off technology against the cost of increased training.

The M203 grenade launcher, seen here attached to an M16, is a useful support weapon for lightly armed special forces and airborne units.

Above: The 7.62mm L7A2 general purpose machine gun is a reliable and very robust weapon.

However, in terms of 'winning the firefight', this takes on a new importance in the light of General S. Marshall's analysis in his book *Men Against Fire*, in which he calculated that only 15 per cent of World War II infantrymen actually fired their weapons in any particular engagement — other experts suggest the slightly higher figure of 25 per cent for some battles. The four rifles being considered by the ACR Program have been submitted by Heckler & Koch of Germany, Steyr of Austria, Colt Industries and the Aircraft Armaments Inc.

The design of the Heckler & Koch G11 is extremely innovative. Its cyclic rate of fire of 600 rounds per minute (rpm) is about the same as a World War II machine gun. However, its three-shot burst mode has a cyclic rate of fire of 2000rpm, ensuring that all three rounds are chambered and fired before the recoiling parts have reached the buffer at the end of the recoil. Consequently, the three rounds are on their way to the target before the marksman's shoulder registers the recoil and the barrel starts to lift. This produces a significantly tighter grouping at 100-300m than three rounds interspersed by recoil shocks.

One unusual feature of the G11 is the 4.92mm (or 4.7mm depending on which system

of measuring calibre is employed) caseless ammunition. At 0.6kg/100 rounds they are a mere quarter of the weight of 7.62mm bullets and are embedded in a solid block of propellant which is completely burnt in the barrel, thereby avoiding the traditional jamming problems associated with cartridge ejection — an excellent attribute for small-unit firefights. The weapon is sealed to prevent the intrusion of water and dirt, with the rounds being packed in 15-round clips and sealed in plastic boxes.

The Commando's short barrel produces a brilliant muzzle flash

Another extremely interesting candidate in the ACR Program is the Steyr-Mannlicher ACR. Superficially, the prototype resembles Steyr's successful AUG bullpup assault rifle in service with the Austrian, Australian, Irish, Omani, New Zealand, Moroccan and Saudi Arabian armed forces. The weapon is 76.5cm long, weighs only 3.22kg when empty and fires 5.56mm saboted sub-calibre flechettes which resemble miniature crossbow bolts. Flechettes demonstrate increased tissue penetration but may lack the stopping power of conventional ammunition. The Steyr, which can be fired in semi-automatic or three-burst mode, has a muzzle velocity of 1490m/sec. In addition, tests have shown the weapon to be extremely rugged, making it ideal for extended operations work.

What are the weapons currently used by special forces around the world? Since 1987, elite British units have been equipped with the SA-80, designed to replace the SLR and 9mm Sterling submachine gun. The weapon has a bullpup design and is capable of automatic and single-shot fire, a definite improvement on the SLR. It has a muzzle velocity of 940m/sec and cyclic rate of fire of between 600-850rpm. It can be fitted with the SUSAT (Sight Unit Small Arms Trilux) optical sight, which enhances performance under poor light conditions, or an image intensifying night sight, though it does not have a controlled-burst capability.

Weighing only 3.23kg, the 5.56mm Colt Commando is lighter than the SA-80 and is likely to remain in limited service with British units such as the SAS. Even with the butt extended the Commando is still only 787mm long, and only two millimetres longer than the SA-80. The Commando can be used in the single shot or full-automatic mode, thus fulfill-

ing the dual functions of assault rifle and submachine gun. As a shortened version of the AR-15 high velocity assault rifle, the Commando's very short barrel produces a brilliant muzzle flash, making it advisable to incorporate a flash suppressor for special forces work.

The 5.56mm and 7.62mm Galil assault rifle is an excellent weapon and is in use with Israeli elite forces. Robust and designed for the sandy environment of the Middle East, the Galil owes much in design to the AK-47. Capable of operating as an automatic or single shot weapon, the Galil rifle has a muzzle velocity of 980m/sec (5.56mm) or 850m/sec (7.62mm) and a cyclic rate of fire of 650rpm. Both models weigh less than 4kg, making them ideal for foot patrols.

Hostage-rescue units sometimes favour .22 or .250 'soft kill' rifles

Sniper rifles have tended to retain the 7.62mm round, which provides stability and good ballistic qualities for long-range shooting. The 7.62mm Parker Hale rifle is designed to ensure a first-round hit on full-sized targets at ranges up to 600m, and an 85 per cent hit rate between 600-900m. Hostage-rescue units sometimes favour .22 or .250 'soft kill' rifles for their low penetration qualities, which are important in situations were the 7.62mm round may exit the felon and then strike a civilian or hostage. Sniper rifles such as the 7.62mm Accuracy

Below: One of the most finely engineered submachine guns in the world, the compact MP5K.

International L96A1 — used by the SAS — are sometimes referred to as 'hard kill' weapons. The L96A1 has an effective range of 1000m and is equipped with a 6x42 telescopic sight, but it can also take large light-gathering scopes such as the Schmidt and Bender 2.5-10x56 telescope. A sniper rifle favoured by Germany's elite GSG 9 counter-terrorist unit is the Heckler & Koch 7.62mm G3 SG/1 rifle. Designed for semi- and full-automatic fire at targets up to 600m, the weapon employs a roller delayed blow-back action to enhance accuracy. Its high cyclic rate of fire (500-600rpm) makes it an ideal support weapon, as well as a sniper rifle.

The SMG has remained a favourite weapon of the counter-terrorist unit

Machine guns, with their rapid rate of fire, have long been used by elite forces throughout the world. The companion weapon to the SA-80, the 5.56mm L86 A1 Light Support Weapon, with a heavier barrel, is now in service with the British Army. The medium 7.62mm L7A2 general purpose machine gun (GPMG) has been retained for the sustained-fire role. Belt-fed, the GPMG combines an effective range of 800-1400m with a high rate of fire (750-1000rpm) and muzzle velocity (838m/sec). The American Army's equivalent of the L86 A1 is the 5.56mm FN Minimi, or M249 Squad Automatic Weapon (SAW), which can be fed from a belt or magazine. With an effective range of 1300m, the M249 was introduced to provide effective fire beyond the 300m range of the M16. There is an airborne/airmobile infantry version which has a sliding stock and shorter barrel, but it is only slightly lighter (6.8kg) than the standard SAW (6.9kg empty; 9.97kg with 200 rounds and bipod). The standard American GPMG is the two-man M60, which has a cyclic rate of fire of 550rpm. The weapon is provided with a

lete. The modern assault rifle is being designed with automatic and short-burst capability to undertake the dual role of rifle and submachine gun. However, the smaller calibre rifles generally lack the stopping power of the 9mm SMG. Other points in the SMG's favour are its small size, extremely high rate of fire — 900rpm for the MP5K compared to 800rpm for the SA-80 for example — and ease of concealment. Overall, these points have ensured that the SMG has remained a favourite weapon of the counter-terrorist unit.

By far the most popular SMGs with elite units are the 9mm Heckler & Koch MP5 series designed for military use, with the MP5K series produced for special operations and counter-terrorist work. The basic MP5A2 has an overall length of 68cm and a weight of just 2.5kg. Capable of firing full-automatic or in three- or five-round bursts — the number of shots is determined by the trigger mechanism at time of manufacture — various versions are manufactured with fixed and retractable stocks. The MP5SD series are silenced weapons which fire bullets at subsonic speeds to minimise muzzle blast and provide various butt-stock configurations (MP5SD2 — fixed stock; MP5SD3 — retractable stock etc.). The short MP5K (32.5cm) series — MP5K, MP5KA1, MP5KA2

stock and integral bipod, but the M122 tripod mount increases the weapon's effective range from 900m to 1800m.

Many weapons experts believe that the submachine gun is becoming militarily obso-

Below: Used by the German counter-terrorist unit GSG 9, the P9S handgun weighs only 1kg loaded.

and MP5KA5 — were designed to be concealed in clothing, in the glove-box of a car or in a briefcase. Several of the shorter configurations can be fitted with laser sights and fired from inside several specially designed briefcases produced by Heckler & Koch themselves.

The 9mm Italian Spectre SMG was designed after a careful analysis of terrorist attacks revealed that the events during the first five seconds of an incident determined whether a target and his bodyguards lived or died. For reasons of safety, most SMGs, including the Uzi, Steyr MPi69 and Beretta Model 12, must be either carried uncocked or carried with the safety catch applied. Bringing the weapon into action to counter a surprise attack can cost the target or his bodyguard those few precious seconds. The Spectre's double-action firing mechanism allows a magazine to be inserted and the weapon cocked. A de-cocking lever can then be applied, inserting a steel block between the hammer and firing pin to prevent an accidental discharge. The weapon is now in the safe position but can be fired with a stronger pressure on the trigger. The Spectre weighs only 2.9kg unloaded, has a length of 35cm and is the only SMG that fires 850rpm with a closed bolt blow-back firing system.

The most popular handgun among elite forces is the High Power

The 9mm Ingram Models 10/11 are no longer manufactured, but they remain the lightest (1.59kg empty) and shortest (22cm) SMGs ever built. The Ingram can be fitted with a suppressor that allows the round to reach its supersonic speed, though it performs less effectively than a silencer. The 9mm Uzi was first manufactured in 1947 and, while compact (64cm), is still very heavy at 3.5kg. Later models include the Mini and Micro-Uzis, which compete with Heckler & Koch's MP5 series in size and weight.

Most submachine guns and handguns fire short 9mm blunt rounds with a low muzzle velocity and good stopping power at ranges below

Left: The US M224 60mm mortar is a lightweight, man-portable weapon which was designed to be used by airborne units and special forces.

100m. Germany's GSG 9 use the excellent Heckler & Koch 9mm P9S. Delta Force and SEAL Team Six used to use the 0.45 Colt Government ACP for its stopping power. Its low muzzle velocity is more than compensated for by its larger bullet. More recently, they have been issued with the double-action 9mm Beretta 92SBF automatic — the US Army's new service pistol. The most popular handgun among elite forces, however, is still the 9mm Browning High Power, which is used by the British, Australian and New Zealand SAS units, the Israelis and the American FBI Hostage-Rescue Team. The Browning has a proven track record and utilises a high capacity 13-round magazine, making it ideal for sustained fire in an anti-terrorist situation.

HAHO allows a soldier to travel up to 24km before touching down

In addition to personal weapons and ammunition, elite units also need a diverse range of specialised equipment to enable them to fulfill their operational requirements. Adequate transportation to and from the theatre of operations has always presented difficulties for commanders throughout history, and this is especially true of special forces and airborne units. Clandestine insertion methods are imperative for formations such as the SAS, who often operate as four-man teams deep behind enemy lines. Specialist high-altitude, low-opening (HALO) parachute techniques allow soldiers to be dropped from heights of around 10,000m and descend silently to their dropping zone (DZ) undetected. Similarly, high-altitude, high-opening (HAHO) parachute methods, where the soldier opens his 'chute immediately after leaving the aircraft, are also used by special forces. HAHO allows a soldier to travel up to 24km before touching down, making it an ideal silent insertion technique.

The aircraft used by special forces for parachute drops are also employed by conventional airborne units. Formations such as the British and Israeli paras, as well as the US 82nd Airborne Division, employ so-called static-line parachuting (in which the men's 'chutes open automatically as they leave the aircraft) as

opposed to freefall techniques. The aircraft used include the Lockheed C-130 Hercules, a four-engined aircraft with a range of 4000km and the capacity to carry 64 paratroops (the US Air Force (USAF) currently operates 520 of these aircraft). In addition, many Hercules are fitted with refuelling probes which can extend their range. The giant American C-141 Starlifter also has an in-flight refuelling capability and can transport 155 paratroops in its fuselage. The Soviet Union, too, has a large airlift capability, possessing as it does over 600 Il-76 Candid heavy transport aircraft, each capable of carrying 140 paratroops. The USSR currently fields no less than seven airborne divisions.

The helicopter is an ideal tool for special forces operations

The helicopter is an ideal, if expensive, tool for special forces operations as no other military vehicle can match its speed and cross-country mobility. There are a number of helicopters which are ideally suited for special forces use including the Bell UH-1N, an airframe devel-

Above: The MC-130 Combat Talon aircraft is a special operations version of the C-130. It is fitted with special avionics for low-level operations.

oped from the famous UH-1 'Huey'. The larger CH-47 Chinook transport helicopter can carry 44 troops and was used recently by the US Marines in the Gulf War; an air-refuellable version was also used to insert SAS and SEAL teams into Iraq and Kuwait. The American Sikorsky corporation produces a number of helicopter models which are in service with the US Marines and other American airborne units. Their massive CH-53 Sea Stallion has an unrefuelled range of 2076km, although this can be extended by means of its air refuelling probe. The UH-60 Black Hawk assault and transport helicopter is the workhorse of the 101st Airborne Division. Capable of carrying 11 fully equipped soldiers, it can also be armed with machine guns and Hellfire anti-tank missiles.

An aircraft which combines the attributes of the helicopter and aircraft is the Bell/Boeing Vertol V-22 Osprey, a twin engine tilt-rotor aircraft currently undergoing evaluation. It is

186

capable of carrying up to 24 troops and will be ideally suited to US Marine Corps (USMC) operations, as they are able to provide rapid and flexible deployment from ship to shore. Due to enter service with the Army and Marines in the early 1990s, the Osprey's versatility means it will undoubtedly also be used for special forces work.

Specialised land vehicles have, since World War II, played an important part in transporting special forces. The Long Range Desert Group patrols in the north African desert demanded rugged vehicles that could carry the required quantities of food, water, ammunition and fuel, as well as personnel, to support their operations. Today, this tradition is continued with such vehicles as Land Rover's series of long-range reconnaissance vehicles, the French ACMAT VLRA and the Israeli M-325 Command Car. Vehicles such as the Land Rover are fully self-contained and are equipped with GPMGs, ammunition containers, radios, smoke

Below: Fast attack vehicles, such as this Wessex Saker, are used by US and British special forces.

Above: Soviet naval infantry storm ashore from an air-cushion vehicle, one of 82 in their armoury.

grenades and camouflage netting, and have ranges in excess of 800km.

Another wheeled vehicle which has enjoyed great success with the American military is the high mobility, multi-purpose wheeled vehicle, or 'Hummer'. Its importance may be judged by the fact that some 40,000 will be purchased by the US Army, with another 11,000 going to the USAF and 14,000 to the USMC. The vehicle's light aluminium body makes it ideal for transportation in the fuselage of a transport aircraft or slung underneath a helicopter — two can be carried by a Chinook, one by a Black Hawk and up to 15 in the fuselage of a C-5 Galaxy aircraft. The Hummer is currently available in 15 different variants including troop carrier, command vehicle and an anti-tank version.

The US Navy currently operates some 65 amphibious vessels

The revolutionary dune buggy-type vehicle employed by American and British special forces has a number of advantages over larger vehicles such as the Jeep and Land Rover: it is easier to conceal and to transport by air, it is more nimble and it presents a smaller target to the enemy. Models such as the Chenworth Fast attack Vehicle (FAV), the Wessex Saker and Longline's Light Strike Vehicle (LSV) have rear-mounted, unenclosed air-cooled engines and can mount a variety of weapons including machine guns, canons and anti-tank missiles. Such vehicles were used to great effect in the recent Gulf War by SAS and SEAL teams to hit targets behind Iraqi lines.

Insertion onto an enemy coastline has long been practised by elite forces, from small teams of the British Special Boat Squadron (SBS) and American SEALs to full-scale invasions such as at D-Day and Iwo Jima in World War II. The US Navy currently operates some 65 amphibious vessels ranging in size from the 'Iwo Jima' class landing platform helicopter (LPH) ships, which can carry 1700 troops, four Harrier fighter aircraft, two CH-46 Sea Knight helicopters, 10 CH-53 helicopters and one UH-1N helicopter, to numerous small utility landing craft. The Soviet Union operates three giant 'Ivan Rogov' class amphibious assault ships, each capable of carrying 520 troops, 20 tanks and five KA-27 Helix naval helicopters.

Both the United States and the Soviet Union also employ numerous hovercraft and landing craft air cushion (LCAC) vessels, the latter being able to carry a variety of cargo including main battle tanks, and can reach speeds of 50-75 knots. These craft have a number of advantages over traditional landing craft vessels: high speeds, ability to travel over water and shore obstacles, very low underwater signatures, high payload capacity and ability to operate from a variety of platforms and bases. Other smaller vessels used by special forces include the two-man Klepper canoe deployed by the SBS and various inflatable commando craft, such as the sub-skimmer made by Submarine Products Ltd. Five metres long and capable of a surface speed of 27 knots, this craft can convert to a mini-submarine and carry up to four divers.

Elite units have earned their fame in battle by the careful selection of the man, his weapons and equipment, and the unit's tactics. Training and combat weld these various elements into an effective fighting force. Highly specialised roles require an even higher degree of selection and training. Competitions and exercises, held by units such as the Royal Marines and British Parachute Regiment, put great emphasis on effective shooting after completing long, exhausting endurance marches. Surprise and

speed are essential to the commando and airborne roles, but are a mere prerequisite to the main task of eliminating the enemy. Night shooting is a stock-in-trade for such units as the SAS and SEALs. Foreign weapons training is an essential skill in Special Force's 'A-Teams', but a general familiarity with weapons can be a great asset to any unit. In the closing stages of the Arnhem battle, for example, isolated areas of the airborne perimeter were only held because British paratroops fought with captured weapons and ammunition. Firearms training is particularly intense for counter-terrorist units. In an average year, the GSG 9 member fires more than 8000 rounds in training, while the walls of the old SAS 'Killing House' were reputed to contain so many bullets that there was a serious risk of lead poisoning.

However, marksmanship and good equipment in themselves do not win battles or rescue hostages; self-discipline and team work are also important. Many elite unit actions defy logical analysis in terms of superior firepower or equipment. To explain the success of the few French legionnaires at Camerone, the Rangers on the beaches of Normandy and Italy, the US Marines in the Pacific, the small Green Beret teams in Vietnam or the British Paras at Goose Green, it becomes necessary to use that more mysterious term: *esprit de corps*.

Below: An amphibious USMC LVTP-7 in Saudi Arabia in January 1991, prior to 'Desert Storm'.

PICTURE CREDITS

Aviation Pictures International
Front Jacket, 40-41, 65, 66, 67, 189;
Brown Packaging 14, 15, 63t, 82, 83, 84t, 84b, 86, 87 , 90-91, 138, 139 , 154-155, 156, 159, 164-165, 180;
Camera Press 23, 27, 90;
Express Newspapers 64;
Ian Hogg 181, 183;
Robert Hunt Library 6-7, 8, 9, 10, 11, 32, 43, 71, 74, 75, 94, 95, 104, 118, 120;
IWM 30, 58, 59, 60-61, 97, 132, 133, 134;
PMA Pictures 2-3, 12-13, 17, 141, 157, 158, 160, 161;
Military Picture Library 56-57;
Robin Adshead 28-29, 37, 38, 92-93, 128-129, 176-177, 179, 184;
Patrick Allen 39;
Peter Russell 187;
Popperfoto 31,34-35,44,46,51,72-73, 106, 108, 109, 115, 142-143, 163;
Press Association 63b;
Rex Features 49, 52, 80-81, 101, 102-103, 105, 110, 113, 121, 140, 144, 146, 173;
Frank Spooner 18-19, 21, 36, 45, 77, 78-79, 98, 116-117, 124, 125, 153, 167, 168, 170-171b, 170-171t, 172, 175, 188;
Sygma 111;
TASS 22, 24-25, 119, 122-123, 126, 127, 182;
Telegraph Library 136-137;
TRH Pictures 16, 20, 33, 54, 55, 68-69, 71b, 76, 130, 131, 148, 150, 151, 174, 186;
US DOD Back Jacket, 100, 145, 147.